Rabbit
Trails

But God... has a plan

୬∞୬

Lois Lee Soto

KingdomEnterprisesInternational
www.KingdomEnterprisesInternational.com
Arlington, Texas

Rabbit Trails - But God... has a plan
Copyright © 2012 Lois Lee Soto

Printed in the United States of America.

For information contact Publisher:
Kingdom Enterprises International Publishing
P.O. Box 122181
Arlington, Texas 76012

www.KingdomEnterprisesInternational.com

ISBN Number 978-0-9741274-4-6

Cover design by Murry Whiteman

DEDICATION

To My Lord and Savior, Jesus Christ.

Thank You for directing me to write this book and for giving me the title and content, but most of all for directing my life.

You, precious Jesus, have been with me on all the "Rabbit Trails" of my life, and always get me back to Your main path. Thank You.

Thank You, precious Jesus, for loving me with your unconditional love.

Thank You for the song You gave me entitled: "Thank You Jesus, For Introducing Me To The Father."

Thank You, Jesus, for sending the Holy Spirit to guide me into all Truth.

John 16:1 AMP
But when He, the Spirit of Truth (the Truth-giving Spirit) comes, He will guide you into all the Truth (the whole, full Truth). For He will not speak His own message [on His own authority]; but He will tell whatever He hears [from the Father; He will give the message that has been given to Him], and He will announce and declare to you the things that are to come [that will happen in the future].

To my precious Rey, who always knew that God would put this book in my heart! You were such a gift from God, to me. Thank you for your unconditional love for me. Heaven is better because you are there.

RABBIT TRAILS

ACKNOWLEDGMENTS

To my dear friends and spiritual leaders, Dr. Bill and Barbara Peters, whose confidence in me has kept me going on this journey? I could not have done this without your love and support. I love you and thank you!

To my children, KJ and Ray, for your love, support, and encouragement, I thank you for your unconditional love. I love you more than words can say!

To my children: Irene, Lucy, Jerry, and Jimmy. I didn't birth you, but you are loved as my children, nonetheless. Thank you for loving me.

To my precious grandchildren: Matthew, Christopher, Amber, Amanda, Michael, Timothy, and Hannah, thank you for your special love. To Candace, thank you for being a Godly wife to Matthew. To Levi, for being the man of God you are for my birthday girl, Amber.

To the grandchildren I inherited: Jerry Jr., Jeanie, Eva, and Robin, with all your spouses and children. Thank you for the joy you brought to the family.

To my great-grandchildren: Mario, Olivia, Daniel, Savannah, Elijah, Simon, Josiah and Ryder, may all my love and prayers for you bear fruit in your life. May you always live for Jesus!

To my sister, Mildred, and brother, Raymond, who hold a special place in my heart. Thank you for your love during good times and bad, and the joy you bring into my life. Thank you, Willie, for loving my sister, and the delight you bring into our family.

To my brothers, Dennis and Eddie, I look forward to really knowing you.

To my dear friend, prayer partner and pal, Vince Carella, thanks for your encouragement and support. Thank you for our friendship and for your son, Nicholas, who has my love and prayers, always.

To Diane Wigstone, for your many awesome talents. They could fill many pages. Thank you for being my publisher! You are a blessing!

To Jessica Jones, for your talent to help me by taking on the laborious job of editing. Thank you.

To Murry Whiteman, your remarkable giftings are so awesome. Your artwork on this book was invaluable. You are such an inspiration. Thank you.

To all of my church family at Angel Fire Christian Center. Thank you for your love and prayers.

To Pastors Kenny and Brenda Gatlin and family, who imparted so very much to me. Thank you for your love and impartation.

To all my friends at Integrity Christian Center. Thank you for your love and prayers.

To Pastor John and Pam McLaughlin, and their church family, for being such a part of my life, thank you.

To all my "relatives" in the Clair families, of which I still remain a part, I love you all. Thank you.

To all my friends and relatives who have so encouraged me over the years. Thank you.

Last, but not least: To Judy, for your selfless love in helping me rear my children during those difficult early years. Thank you!

To all the ones who have gone on before me:

My precious husband, Rey; you were my "North." Thank you for your unconditional love.

My daughter, Zoe Leeta, who is having such a good time with Jesus. I hear your infectious laugh! Thank you for your enduring love and the grandchildren you gave me.

My Mama and Daddy Potter, who loved me as their own. Thank you for your love and example. I am eternally grateful. I will see you in your mansion over there.

To the Cosper family, who welcomed me into the family, and accepted me as their own, through Mama Potter. Thank you to those who have gone home and to the ones who remain here, as well.

Grandson, John: Thank you for your love and the joy you brought into my life. Enjoy Heaven, John.

My birth parents, Loyd and Vessie. Thank you for bringing me into this world. I will see you again, someday, inside the pearly gates.

To all my grandparents, and my baby sister, Lena.

To Dad and Mom Clair and all those in the Clair families, who have gone for their reward.

I am so grateful you all knew Jesus and I have the assurance I will see you again, someday.

CONTENTS

INTRODUCTION

The Lord asked me to write this book to record many of the lessons I have learned in life along with the recounting of some of the many blessings God has given to me. This effort is an act of obedience on my part, not my talent.

My ultimate goal is to help others. I truly realize that we all have gifts and callings that can still be as real today as they were when we first received them. God does not put a timetable on our callings, and often there is a major time difference between our "calling" and our being "set apart" for the work that He has for us to do. I am called to write what God reveals to me, for such a time as this.

In order to explain how I got to where I am now, I need to give you a little bit of background.

I was born in Thomas, Oklahoma to Loyd Franklin and Vessie Jane Stevens. I was the second of four children. In my early years, Thomas had a population of eleven-hundred plus residents and contained thirteen churches. My great- grandparents were one of two families that started the settlement.

I carry in my genes many different nationalities. My paternal grandfather had English and Native American of the Sioux tribe in his ancestry. My paternal great- grandmother was Pennsylvania Dutch, and I can remember her quite well, which is where I got my Dutch and German blood. My maternal grandmother was French-Canadian and my maternal grandfather was Scot-Irish.

They chose to name me Lois Lee. Thank you for the name you gave me. According to The Name Book by Dorothy Astoria, the meanings and associated Scriptures are awesome!

Lois: "Desired" & "Established In Truth"
Lee: "From The Sheltered Place" and "Gracious"

2 Sam. 22:29 NKJV
"For You are my lamp, O LORD; The LORD SHALL enlighten my darkness.

Rom. 8:16 NKJV
16 The Spirit Himself bears witness with our spirit that we are children of God.

I realize the enemy tried to kill me on more than one occasion, but God said, "NO." I had scarlet fever when I was only a few months old, as my mother also had it. I know it is not supposed to be possible to remember that far back, but I can see myself in that back bedroom in bed with my mother and we were both very sick. I remember the room and the position of the bed, adjacent to a window, with the shades drawn in an attempt to keep out the light. I do not understand the significance of my remembering that, but I am sure God has a purpose. Actually, although I have been blessed to have an excellent memory throughout my whole life, when I was thirty-two years old, the enemy tried to destroy my memory. God, again, said," NO! I will not allow it!" I will expound on that experience in another chapter in this book.

When I was 4 years old, I was in a head-on collision. There were no seat belts in those days, so I flew from the back seat through the windshield of the car. I had a large gash on my head (which left a scar), but otherwise, I had no signs of injury. That scene has never left my consciousness. I can still see it now, as I saw it then.

But God…has a plan

When I was around five years old, I had my first encounter with The Lord, but I was unaware of the significance of it at that time. I was from the side of the family that was un-churched. My great aunt invited me to Sunday school in my hometown and I went. It must have been an Easter Sunday, because it was the message of the Cross.

I did not understand the concept, but I fell in love with this man named Jesus, because of all the wonderful things He did and the realization that He did them for me. I really wanted to meet Him, but didn't think He was in town. But I loved Him, loved Him, loved Him. So much so, that when the teacher asked us to bring our pennies to Jesus, I took every penny from the pocket of my little cotton dress and gave them all to this wonderful man, Jesus. It seemed the least that I could do for such a loving person.

Back then, you could get a lot of candy for a penny, but that did not matter to me at that moment in time, as I had this overwhelming desire to give all that I had to Jesus. I still enjoy that memory, and my desire to give has never waned.

My parents divorced when I was five and so many things happened in my life during the next four years that were not good. I lived in seven different homes during those four years, including living in our little rented house with my younger brother when our father was not around.

My brother is two and half years younger than I am and I felt responsible for him during that period when we were alone; he went everywhere with me. I still have a special love for my "little" (now 6'1") brother! We learned to like a lot of cheese and crackers and we both like them to this day!

During those years, I know the Holy Spirit protected my heart, for in spite of all the upheaval, and unspeakable incidents, it never imbedded in my heart.

When I was 6 years old, I lived in at least three of those seven homes. One that still stands out in my mind was a nice couple who lived in a lovely mobile home park in New Mexico. I had grown up in an environment of alcohol and gambling, so playing cards was nothing new to me. Each afternoon, the woman with whom I was living had female friends over and they sat around the table playing cards. The minute they started, an unrest that I cannot describe came over me, and I would run through the park as though the devil himself was after me. I wanted to get as far away from that house as I could. This happened each time the women came to play cards!

I was a mild-mannered child and not given to such behavior. I had learned at a young age that if I wanted to have a roof over my head, I needed to be obedient. My behavior was completely at odds with my temperament, and neither the couple nor my father could understand it. My father had to remove me from that home, because I kept running away each afternoon, though my behavior was completely docile the rest of the time. When I first saw Tarot cards as an adult, I recognized them as the cards with which these women were playing. So, even then, I discerned the evil spirit associated with that activity. The gift of discerning of spirits has come to my rescue many times over the years.

I will fast forward past the ages of six to eight, as some of my experiences are not ones that I want to dwell upon or relive. They would not be uplifting to me or to you. Suffice it to say, they were not good! I will say that my father or mother never abused me in any manner, but were not always around to offer me protection, either. I was never subjected to beatings, but the form of abuse that I did suffer was not obvious to others. I was too young to recognize it as sexual abuse in the worst form and mistook it for love. God protected my spirit and my soul.

I was nine and a half years old when a wonderful Christian couple, Jess and Eura Lee Potter, asked if I could come to live with them on the farm and be their daughter. My father gave his consent to this, so I finally had a permanent home. That was May 3, 1942. It was a very memorable day in my life! The Potters were "poor folk" in the eyes of the world, but they were "rich" in Heaven's roster.

During my first Sunday service at the little Assembly of God Church in Thomas, Oklahoma I accepted Jesus Christ into my heart.

That was May 10, 1942, which was Mothers' Day! That was without a doubt the most important day of my life! I finally understood that the Jesus I had heard about four years prior could actually take residence in my heart!

I then began to "tarry" for the Baptism of The Holy Spirit. We did not understand back then that one did not need to "tarry" for the Baptism in The Holy Spirit, (any more than we had to go to Jerusalem to receive it) so we "tarried." I did not have to wait long, however, and I received the Baptism of the Holy Spirit, evidenced by speaking in other tongues! I was also water baptized down at the river by our Pastor who later became the Presbyter of our District. I still have a picture of me in my little white dress standing in the river after I had been baptized.

After I went to live with my new Mama and Daddy, the first thing they did was take me down to the local department store. They bought me two new pairs of shoes: one for school and one for Church. I had been going barefoot except for the cowboy boots I got for Christmas when I was six years old. I was still wearing them at age nine. I had outgrown them and my heel was resting on the uppers when I put them on. But they were mine and I loved them. I gave them up the day I got my new shoes.

Recently, in the night hours, as I was listening to God I said, "Lord why did I continue to want to wear those old worn out boots?" He said, "They were familiar, and you liked them." He went on to say, "That is how so many of my children are today. They continue in the familiar and become so comfortable with it, even when they have outgrown that stage in their walk with Me, they are not willing to step into My new (anointing) that I have prepared for them." Whoa!

That Fall, just after my tenth birthday, I had a remarkable experience. I had just walked the two miles home from my little country school where I was in fifth grade and went to my room to change out of my school clothes, as I always did. I can still see that scene and that experience. I see my little bed with the lovely quilt Mama had made me for a bedspread with all its bright colors. As I stood there, suddenly in the corner of my room, the devil

14

appeared in a red suit with a pitchfork. I recognized him by his appearance! In this open vision I reached on my bed, a shotgun was lying there, and I picked it up, pointed it at the devil, and blew him totally away. At that moment a loud authoritative voice from above thundered, "Go ye into all the world and preach the gospel to every creature!"

Suddenly, the scene changed and I was just standing there in my room. Of course, there wasn't actually a shotgun on my bed.

That open vision has stayed with me these many years and I can still see and hear it today, as though it were then. I have not physically gone into the entire world, but I have sown seed into others that have gone into "all the world."

I did not fully understand that vision at the time, but as I shared it with my elders, they immediately interpreted it to mean that I had a call to preach. Our Pastor even had me "preach" several times. Those were short sermons! Being behind a church pulpit did not appear to be my life calling after all, though I do speak on occasion. So that vision was put on the back burner, waiting on God. Nevertheless, the vision remained in me and I always made sure over the years to support ministries and missionaries. I came to realize, by the Spirit of God, that this was the primary way in which I was to preach the gospel. The confirmation was the way the Lord thrust me into the business world. That was another miracle! I will write about that later.

Mama suffered with migraines and various illnesses since she had previously had two miscarriages and was unable to have children. That was the reason they wanted me so badly. I was truly their daughter! My middle name was the same as Mama and I also had her hair and eye color.

I came to realize, as Mama did, that God had chosen to use me in the gift of healing, because when I laid my hands on her and prayed, her pain would disappear immediately. God has continued to use me in that gift over the years and I have witnessed dramatic healings, as well as creative miracles, performed by God using me as the delivery person.

But God...has a plan

I quit high school when I was fifteen years old. I was in my junior year and going to a private Christian school. One of the teachers had promised the class that our test would be on a certain day, knowing that we girls always prepared just before the test. She then had it earlier than she had announced to us, so we were unprepared. She thought it was funny, as though she had played a joke on us. When we complained, she then agreed to do a re- test and give us that grade. She changed her mind about that as well, saying she would average the two grades. I felt that she had lied to me and I could not trust her anymore. At that point I made the decision to quit school. (I have always had a very strong opinion about telling the truth, as my children can all attest. Do not ever lie to me!)

Of course that was a bad decision, but Mama and Daddy supported me in it. Back then not everyone understood the value of a good education.

I married Bill, a twenty-one year old Spirit-filled Christian man, when I was sixteen. Our courtship had happened primarily through correspondence, so we did not know each other as well as we might have otherwise. That was not unusual for that time and place, as mutual friends had introduced us.

After we were married we started our life together on a farm in Kansas. We had a precious daughter, Zoe Leeta, a year later when I was seventeen. Bill had decided to go to college in Oklahoma, so we moved back to my hometown, and the same Doctor that had delivered me seventeen years earlier delivered Zoe Leeta! He always called her his first grandbaby!

She was a delightful and happy baby and Mother and Daddy Potter doted on her. Daddy Potter talked to her so much that she first spoke at six months old, even before she began walking two months later. How shocked we were that she had formed complete words, mimicking her granddaddy. Unfortunately, she had colic in the evenings and was very fussy. We always took her to church anyway and our Pastor would preach, holding her in one arm and his Bible with the other. She never cried when he was holding her! The anointing calmed her. He really loved her and had officiated over her dedication to the Lord. He was a wonderful man of God. Zoe Leeta is with Jesus now, since February 2005, and I miss her so much. Sometimes I can hear her contagious laughter and realize how much she is enjoying Heaven.

But God...has a plan

My husband, Bill, had developed tuberculosis early in our marriage and was hospitalized for long periods. He was a veteran so we had to live wherever they sent him for treatment, if it was possible. My children were not able to be with their father during most of those years. They could only look at him through the glass windows of the hospital.

I worked at whatever I could find to do during

those early years, but in January 1956 I had an urging in my spirit to apply for a job I saw advertised in an Oklahoma City newspaper. It was in a new car dealership. They needed an Office Manager (a position for which I had no knowledge), and I know it was God that sent me there! I was very shy and would never have been so presumptuous as to even apply for such a position, so I know it was Holy Spirit boldness!

I got the job, but what about the work I was expected to do? Remember, I had quit school. I had not even taken bookkeeping in high school!

My first day on the job, they brought out all the journals, ledgers and documents and placed them on my desk. I opened the first journal, and at that instant I had a revelation of the whole system. Knowledge about how it all worked just dropped into my spirit. It was as though I had been doing this for years! It was truly a "download" of knowledge of a complicated accounting system, unique only to the auto business. I was in the Automobile Business for the next fifty-plus years, had my own dealership at one time, and worked in high- level positions for other dealers. I also did work as a trouble-shooter at the request of various automobile manufacturers, at the dealership level. I was said to be one of the best in my field. God told me I could take the credit as long as I always remembered to give Him the glory. I never forgot that Word.

In 1959, Bill was due for surgery the second time with only a ten percent chance of survival. I laid hands on him before I left his room the night before surgery and prayed for a miracle. I then asked him to make sure they did new x-rays the next morning before they operated. He agreed, and they did new x-rays that revealed that the hole in his lung was totally closed and there was no sign of tuberculosis, so the surgery was cancelled. They later transferred him to California, not knowing what else to do with him, as they could not yet acknowledge he was healed and whole!

The VA had a hospital in California at that time where he would be allowed to be outside, which made him available to our children. In less than two years, the doctors finally decided that he was indeed free of tuberculosis and discharged him. During that time, he was able to regain most of his strength.

We had been married about 12 years when he came home permanently. We were married for nineteen-plus years and had three beautiful children: Zoe Leeta, Ray Alan and Karla June. Due to all of circumstances and turmoil in our lives, we had grown far apart, in completely opposite directions, so we divorced. Bill was, and is, a fine man and a great father to our children. He soon remarried, and he and his lovely wife now reside in his home state of Kansas, which fulfilled the desire of his heart.

But God...has a plan

I married Rey Soto in December of 1970. Rey had not yet become a Christian when I married him, and some thought it would not work, but I knew in my heart that it was the will of God. I never "preached" to Rey, but I continually prayed for him. I did not try to "get him saved" because he would have done anything for me. I knew that it had to be God alone to bring Rey to an encounter with Him. We had a wonderful, glorious marriage and after seven-and-a-half years, God did what

19

He does best and put Rey in the position of hearing and receiving at the World Convention of The Full Gospel Business Men's Fellowship International (FGBMFI). His encounter with God was truly a divine appointment.

Rey took off for God like a super-sonic fighter plane and served God passionately the rest of his life. His gifts were varied and dynamic, but he held firmly to his message from God that everyone should be filled with the Holy Spirit with the evidence of speaking in tongues and interpretation. His book, "Have You Received The Holy Spirit Since You Believed", has been distributed worldwide. He never sold his book, but gave it to many ministries for distribution. He had a passion for Jesus that I had never witnessed before.

Thousands received the Holy Spirit through Rey's ministry. He also realized many healings through the laying on of hands during those twenty- five years. He went home to be with Jesus in October of 2003. He had finished his course and kept the faith.

But God...has a plan

I have since left my home of thirty-five years in Rancho Palos Verdes, California, in obedience to the Father, and relocated to the Simi Valley, CA area to be involved in ministry with dear friends and serve on the Board of Directors of their church, Angel Fire Fellowship. I also serve on the Board of their non-profit humanitarian organization, International Children's Aid Network, Inc. (ICAN). We are building children's villages for orphans and other vulnerable children in sub-Saharan Africa. This is now the passion of my heart!

That is my life in a nutshell, although there is not a nutshell big enough to hold all of my experiences with God!

But God...has a plan

I now want to cover Biblical lessons that I have learned over the years, as well as some of the experiences I have had. My intent and purpose is that they will help you and encourage you in your walk with the Lord. If even one of my experiences that I will share can help you, then this book will not have been in vain.

We experience many twists and turns on this pathway of life, many of which we have not planned. If we stay close to the Lord, He will see that we always get back to our main path.

The Lord gave me the title of this book as I was lying in a hospital bed having a battery of tests. I was just carrying on a conversation with Him, as I do very frequently. I was inquiring of Him why He so often leads me down "rabbit trails" when I speak. He didn't really answer my question; He simply stated, "that is the name for your book: Rabbit Trails." I know, of course, that He is also in control of all our "rabbit trails."

I have so far learned many lessons over my lifetime and I know I will learn many more as I go forward with God's plan for my life. "Where He leads me I will follow", as the old song goes.

So come along with me, and let us examine some of the "rabbit trails" of my life!

But God...has a plan

21

One thing I ask: please read the associated scriptures along with the content, as this is probably the most important part of the book! I have placed them in their entirety, rather than just references, to make it easier for you.

CHAPTER ONE

OBEDIENCE

I have to admit it was very difficult for me to select which subject to cover first: forgiveness, love or obedience. They all are so important and can hardly be separated! Since forgiveness and love are themselves an act of obedience, I believe obedience must be first. Obedience is paramount to our walk with Jesus. If we are not obedient to His voice, we should expect nothing!

1 Sam 15:22 KJV
So Samuel said: "Has the Lord as great delight in burnt offerings and sacrifices, As in obeying the voice of the Lord? Behold, to obey is better than sacrifice, And to heed than the fat of rams."

The Lord has shown me the importance of instant obedience. It can be a matter of life and death. Let me share an example of this and how The Father taught me this lesson.

On this particular night we had gone to bed after a busy weekend and Rey had dropped off to sleep, but I was still reading. It was 11:20 p.m. when the Lord spoke to my spirit and said pray for "B." (I will just use an initial here, for privacy reasons) I questioned the Lord, to be sure I heard Him clearly, that it was really the "B" that he meant. He assured me that it was that young man. God's voice was very emphatic, so I immediately started interceding in the Spirit. I was in strong intercession for about twenty minutes. Finally, the Spirit of Intercession lifted and I went back to bed.

The young man's father would stop by our dealership occasionally and he was there the following week. He was a close friend that Rey had led to the Lord, so it was not unusual for him to stop in when he was in the area. After I greeted him, I inquired of his son. He said he had not heard from him in several years, because his son was into drugs and hanging out in the drug-infested section of San Francisco. He was curious as to why I had asked, and I merely explained he had been on my heart. He said that he would let me know if he did hear from him. Approximately three weeks later I received word from the father that his son was in the local mental hospital. He went on to tell me that his son "B" had been on the street in a neighboring city and, while high on drugs, he had pulled a knife on a police officer. They were within their right to use deadly force, but instead they managed to subdue him. He was sent to the institution for treatment, as they could see he was suffering from brain damage due to the use of drugs.

Upon checking the date and time, he told me that it had happened, I realized that it was at the exact time that God had me praying! God spoke to me and said, "I allowed you to get the whole story this time, to impress upon you that immediate obedience can be a matter of life or death!" That lesson has really made an impact on my life of obedience! Obedience, in itself, is not always enough. It must be instant obedience! Today, that man is a follower of Jesus Christ.

Obedience on a daily basis can change your life and the lives of others. Rey and I had been married for just over seven years. It was March of 1978. Rey asked me if I wanted to go to Laguna Beach and stay at the penthouse room of a local beach hotel. I said, "sure!" He made the reservations and told me they had requested we send a check for the first night, to hold the reservation. I sat down at my desk to type out the check, but my spirit checked me so I put it off for another time! Each time I started to type it, I was checked in my spirit. I was never able to prepare the check.

The same month we received an invitation to visit Oral Roberts Ministry in Tulsa. Rey was not in the least interested in visiting them. I suggested to him that if we went to Tulsa, it would also give us an opportunity to visit Mother Potter in Oklahoma. He said okay, if that is what I would enjoy. I sent in the   confirmation card   to OREA/ORU. We were scheduled for the end of July, 1978. Well, July 3 came very quickly. On that morning, Rey suggested we get an early start to the beach for the week we had planned. I looked at him and quietly said, "I didn't send in the check to the hotel." His response was, "well, I guess we will enjoy our week here in our own spa." Based on that, there was no reason to get up early.

Rey was looking at the newspaper and saw an ad for the Full Gospel Business Men's Fellowship International meeting that was being held in Anaheim, California, and asked if I knew what it was about and what time it was starting. He was curious about it because it said "business men." Rey was a motivational speaker and trainer, in addition to being a businessman, so the ad got his attention. He was not even thinking about what the word "Full" meant in their name! I suggested that he should call the local bookstore, as they would probably have all the information. He asked if I would call, but instead I just got him the number so that he could make the call. I was led off the Lord to allow Rey to follow up on this without my assistance. He called and they gave him the information, and after the call he made the remark that they answered the phone oddly, as they answered with "Praise the Lord" (I had given him the number for the Christian bookstore). We laughed about the way they answered the phone, but they had given him the information.

"Well," Rey informed me, "it opens at noon, so if we want to be there by then, we could leave now and have breakfast at Belisles" (Our favorite restaurant in the area, which is not far from the Anaheim Convention Center). I knew in my spirit that God was doing something and I needed to listen very closely. We got ready and went to breakfast, as he had suggested.

When we arrived at the Anaheim Convention Center, Rey parked in the rear near the California Room entrance. He was familiar with the facility, as we had often been a part of Recreational Vehicle Shows there, and we dealers had always used that back entrance. We made our way through the back to the front. A few people were scurrying around setting up things and Rey wanted to know why all those people were standing outside the front door! The man that appeared to be in charge responded that they were waiting for the doors to open. Really! We were already inside! The man asked Rey if we were registered, to which he responded, "registered for what?" The man explained they were having a convention

(Rey still did not even know what kind of convention it was). Rey asked me if I would go register us, which I did. What he did not know at the time was that I had registered us for the whole week! We had tickets for all the breakfasts and certain special functions, but there had been no tickets left for the Demos Shakarian Luncheon, or the Pat Robertson dinner. Rey really liked Pat, as we had watched him on "The 700 Club." He went back to the registration desk and tried to get those tickets, but to no avail. They were sold out! He was not very happy about that! Once the doors were opened to the public, it became a flurry of activity and there were people everywhere! We hung out for a while and then left for home.

As we were leaving, I mentioned that the breakfast the next day was at 7 am... Rey informed me that he was not going to get up early to be in Anaheim at seven, because he was on vacation! That was strange to me, because Rey was always an early riser. Every time I started to say something I heard that still voice say, "keep still." It took about an hour to get home and I did not say one word the entire trip. Keeping your mouth shut for an entire hour is no easy task! Rey talked the whole time and I just smiled, nodded and listened.

As we pulled into our driveway, Rey said, "Well, I guess we can go to that breakfast in the morning." Since Rey was the early riser in the family, the responsibility to make it to the breakfast on time rested completely on my shoulders. I said, "great," so I could not change my mind when 5 a.m. came around!

I got up early, because I knew I had to pack my things for the week ahead. Rey laughed and said, "Are you taking all of that? The only way we will stay is if we can find a room really close, and you know that they said they were all sold out!" I responded, "Oh, we will find a room." He threw in one shirt because he truly did not believe we would be staying. I packed for the whole week! We went to the breakfast.

After breakfast, Rey laughingly asked me where I thought w e should l o o k for a room. At that time, there were only two hotels close to the Anaheim Convention Center: Inn at The Park and Quality Inn. We walked into Inn at The Park since we were closer to it now. Rey walked up and asked to register for a room.

The clerk asked for our name, he gave it and she started to look it up and he said, "It won't be in there." She replied with an incredulous tone, "You don't have a reservation?" Rey replied "no" and she slammed her book shut, replying, " We h a v e b e e n s o l d o u t f o r over six months!" Rey asked, "Where would you suggest looking?" "Across the street at the Quality Inn and then make the circle about 15 miles larger!"

I looked up the number for the Quality Inn at the pay phone and handed Rey the number and the coin. I knew in my spirit that this was all something he had to do. I also knew that it had to be that particular hotel because he had made it clear it had to be close to the convention center or we were not staying!

He called and they told him two cancellations had just come in, and although they had a waiting list, since he was on the phone, he could have his choice of the king suite or two doubles. He told them that he would take the king and they informed him that he had to be there within ten minutes. That was not a problem, since we were just across the street. We went over and checked in and Rey then decided he had better go back home and pack his suitcase for the week, which he did, while I rested. God is good!

I still think, even now, that the clerk at Inn at The Park might have found our name in her register if Rey had not said anything. We serve a big God!

After Rey returned with his packed suitcase, we were just wandering around looking at all the display booths and decided to go into the bookstore. At that moment, the Lord spoke to me and said, "Go to the ticket counter and get the tickets for the Demos Shakarian Luncheon and the Pat Robertson Banquet." I whirled around and over my shoulder I said, "I'll be right back," as I walked away. Rey asked me where I was going and I responded as I was walking away, "to get tickets for the luncheon and banquet." He laughed and said something like, "sure you will!"

I walked up to the registration counter and told the girl what I wanted and she informed me that no tickets were available, as they had been sold out for over six months. They had a long waiting list if I wanted to add my name to it. I hesitated, because I knew that I had heard clearly from the Holy Spirit. At that moment the girl at the opposite counter, who had not heard our conversation, handed her an envelope and said, "Here is a cancellation." In this envelope were tickets for all the functions, including the luncheon and the banquet. She looked at the envelope and looked at me, looked at the envelope again and looked back at me, then responded, "Oh well, you are here, so I guess you can have them!" And took out the tickets I needed. I paid for them and left rejoicing in my heart. As I approached Rey, I waved the tickets and he was astounded! He could not understand how I pulled that off! He had not yet come to understand spiritual things!

That Fourth of July was very pleasant and the speakers were anointed. The next morning we again went to the breakfast, then browsed the displays again; early afternoon we looked at the program to see what we wanted to attend. Rey was interested in a "Success in the Business World" teaching being held by Charles Capps. When we got there, the line stretched down the hallway and Rey did not think any speaker could be so good that he would be willing to stand in the hallway to listen, so we left.

He was browsing through the "menu," as he called it, and saw "Baptism in the Holy Spirit" by Enoch Christopherson, Mayor of Turlock, California. He said, "I wonder what this is?" To which I responded, "Do you want to go and find out?" He wanted to go and sit in the back so we could leave if we were so inclined. We were late and the meeting was well under way, as Mayor Christopherson was just finishing his teaching. The Spirit of God was heavy in the room. Mayor Christopherson then asked everyone to kneel at his or her chair, so we knelt to pray. A man from Texas came by and put his hand (not gently) on top of Rey's head. The next thing I knew, Rey was speaking in tongues. Rey became born-again and Spirit-filled all at once. July 5, 1978 ended up being the most important day of Rey's life! He always referred to it as his "birthday." It was beautiful. He was never the same. He was so passionate for the Lord. He later came to understand why a person would stand in the hallway to hear a word from our spiritual brother, Charles Capps. Everything has a time and season!

I was so happy that I had learned to be obedient to the still small voice, because it can change circumstances and lives. Obedience is the prime ingredient in our walk with God! I have no doubt of that fact!

Well...remember when I told you that we had been invited to Tulsa to visit Oral Roberts University? When we got back to the office from the FGBMFI convention, many things started to happen. We had received the invitation showing the date and time that we were supposed to be in Tulsa. It was July 28th. Only three weeks away! It could not have been timelier, because even though Rey had just experienced something wonderful, he was not sure exactly what it all meant. God had his course laid out in advance.

The teaching Brother Oral gave those few days we were in Tulsa was on the Baptism in the Holy Spirit. It was beautiful! Rey now had a foundation for his experience. In September we were at another FGBMFI convention, this time in Palm Springs, and Rey paid all the expenses for two couples to go with us, because he wanted them to get what he had. Each couple was close friends of ours. It was a glorious weekend, as both couples went forward for prayer.

We were also blessed with a beautiful grandson that weekend. Christopher was born into the world on September 24, 1978, shortly after we had returned to our hotel room and I talked to my daughter, Zoe Leeta, who was on the delivery room table at Little Company of Mary Hospital. God is soooo good!

We received an invitation to visit the 700 Club in Virginia Beach, Virginia, so in October Rey was submerged in deep teaching, once again. I believe that he received more during the three months after he was born again than most receive the first three years, or even more!

Rey then w r o t e a teaching workbook entitled: "God's Word...Your Success". He was later led by God to put together a teaching on the baptism in the Holy Spirit entitled, "Have You Received the Holy Spirit Since You Believed?" He was convinced that people should be taught about the Holy Spirit prior to receiving, when possible, so that the devil could not steal it away. Father God also taught him the importance of interpreting your prayer language, as the Holy Spirit wills. He ministered far and wide using this mandate from God. He put together a pamphlet on the subject in both English and Spanish to make it easy for others to minister. He was avid about his call, in spite of opposition.

I think back to that March and realize that if I had not been obedient to the Holy Spirit and had gone ahead and made those reservations in Laguna Beach, how it could have altered the path God wanted us to travel. Let me say it again: obedience is a primary thing! His plans for our good are foiled without obedience.

In 1981 we went to Philadelphia for the FGBMFI World Convention. It was an amazing convention that year, and Rey received vindication for teaching the baptism of the Holy Spirit with interpretation of spiritual languages. Certain men in the group had come against him for teaching interpretation, but he knew it was of God and continued to teach w h a t G o d h a d shown him to teach. They had ordered him to quit teaching on the subject and he said that he would pray about the matter. They informed him that he did not need to pray about it, because they said to stop. He knew that was not right, even though he was still young in the Lord.

He never stopped doing what God ordained him to do, in spite of the opposition.

That July in Philadelphia, Brother Oral preached his message on the same subject: praying in one's private prayer language and interpreting. It was Brother Robert's "Hinds Feet" teaching. No one ever asked Rey to stop teaching on that subject again! At the Philadelphia convention, we would go down to the cavernous basement at five o'clock p.m. each day to pray for the evening service. There were about 20 to 30 of us in the prayer team. One evening at four p.m. the Lord told me to go down to the basement.

I reminded Him that it was only four o'clock and we did not meet until five o'clock. Imagine! Aren't we foolish sometimes? He let me know He was aware, but He wanted me to go down there now. I got up from my seat in the auditorium, and proceeded to go downstairs. It was eerily quiet!

I sat down in one of the chairs and in a few moments a teenager came through on his skateboard. He stopped to talk to me. He had seen everyone meeting there on a prior evening and was curious to know what we were doing there every day. I explained to him that we prayed for the meeting and for people to accept Jesus. I asked him if he knew Jesus. He said no, not really. I asked him if he would like to know Jesus and he said yes, he would!

I led him to the Lord that afternoon before any of the other team members came down. He was a fourteen-year-old boy that needed the Lord and God had sent me to the basement early - just for him! He was aglow as he skated off that night as a born-again creation with a new, little Bible in his hands. I was so grateful that

I had been obedient to the Lord that afternoon. I have thought of him many times over the years and prayed that God would fulfill His plan for his life. I can still envision him with his blond mop of hair, riding his skateboard, sent by God to meet me on that muggy July day in 1981, in Philadelphia. We serve an awesome God!

Another incidence of obedience occurred in Tulsa, Oklahoma while we were attending Kenneth Hagin's Camp Meeting in the summer of 1982. We had decided to go for Haagen Dazs ice cream with some friends of ours: Dave and Jan. It was during the noon break and the Haagen Dazs ice cream parlor was all the way across town from the Tulsa Convention Center where the Camp Meeting was held. Dave was a Haagen Dazs lover, so it was going to be a treat for him! When we got near the location, we decided that we should have a bite of lunch first. There was a restaurant close to the ice cream parlor, so we stopped in there.

We had a nice lunch and as one of the bus boys was bringing us more refreshing drinks, Rey asked him if he knew Jesus. He said that he had heard of him, but knew little of him. My husband then asked him if he would like to know him personally. He responded with an emphatic, "yes!" Rey then led him in the salvation prayer by using the little booklet Dave had written with another man, which explained both salvation and the baptism in the Holy Spirit. As soon as he had accepted Jesus, Rey led him right into Holy Spirit baptism.

You should have seen the change in the countenance of this young man. Rey advised him that he should share what had happened with someone.

He immediately stopped one of his fellow workers, another bus boy, and we were amazed at what came out of his mouth, as they were not the words we had used in leading him to Christ. He said, "I have just received Jesus, the Most High God, into my heart!" What a precious statement.

He then told us that he was from Bangladesh and they have many gods, but none like Jesus! Rey promised him a Bible, and although we were flying out to Dallas the next morning so that Rey could give a testimony at a FGBMFI meeting, Rey made a special trip and gave him his Bible. He said he would go the Camp Meeting service that evening and, although Rey and I would not be there, he could connect with Dave and Jan. We never saw him again, as he'd said, "I must go back to my country and tell my people about Jesus!" Dave and Jan said he indeed was at the service that evening and reiterated his decision to go back to his native land.

When we got back to Tulsa from Dallas two days later, we discovered that he had already left to return to Bangladesh. We take so much for granted here in America about the Gospel of Jesus Christ, but here was this brand new convert that was willing to give up his job in America, a land of promise, to return to a country of poverty, in order to share the Gospel of Jesus Christ with his people! Just listening to the small inner voice of Holy Spirit and stopping for a bite of lunch before ice cream had brought about this miraculous conversion.

God has divine appointments for us to keep every day when we are listening! I believe that Rey has met many people from Bangladesh since he has been in Heaven that are there because of this divine appointment. Keeping God's divine appointments will always bring Blessings to you and others!

RABBIT TRAILS

CHAPTER TWO

FORGIVENESS

At first I started to share about forgiveness with you first, because it is my favorite. But then of course I realized that obedience is the primary thing. Forgiveness must always follow obedience anyway, as it is a commandment we need to obey! Forgiveness is a foundational principle of God's Word, without which you can't ever see nor be able to carry out all of the other blessings and gifts that God has for you. Without forgiveness, you will find it impossible to love the way that God requires you to love. Unforgiveness can block your healing and makes it impossible to be obedient, since being in unforgiveness is, in itself, disobedience.

My precious Mother Potter taught me about the importance of forgiveness immediately after I became Born Again and Spirit Filled. She was the first person with whom I had shared my molestation experiences. My parents, grandparents and siblings did not have any knowledge of the events that had happened to me in my young life by people that were supposed to love me. So Mother Potter taught me about forgiveness. By forgiving, those bad experiences had no hold on me and could not hinder me as I grew. She explained that we are to forgive the people involved, but also distance ourselves from them.

I am so grateful that I learned forgiveness at such a young age; it now comes very naturally for me to walk in forgiveness. I must make the choice not to become offended, even when taking offense is the easiest option and seems justified. Taking offense is the precursor to un-forgiveness. I believe God endows us with a special grace when we choose to walk in forgiveness. It is a door opener for many of God's blessings! Look back over instances in your own life and I am sure you will clearly see exactly what I am talking about!

Neh 9:17b NASU
But You are a God of forgiveness, Gracious and compassionate, Slow to anger and abounding in lovingkindness; And You did not forsake them.

Ps 130:3-4 NASU
If You, LORD, should mark iniquities, O Lord, who could stand? But there is forgiveness with You, That You may be feared.

Dan 9:9 NASU
"To the Lord our God belong compassion and forgiveness, for we have rebelled against Him

Matt 26:28 AMP
For this is My blood of the new covenant, which
[ratifies the agreement and] is being poured out for
many for the forgiveness of sins.

These scriptures give us an insight as to who God is and His unfailing forgiveness to His children. This is for our benefit, as an example of who we should be in God. This is our blueprint. This is the handprint God wants to put on our heart, so we can walk in His path. He is our supreme example! As each of our fingerprints are unique to us individually, so is God's handprint on our hearts, because we are each unique to Him.

Luke 1:77-79 AMP
To bring and give the knowledge of salvation to His people in the forgiveness and remission of their sins. Because of and through the heart of tender mercy and loving-kindness of our God, a Light from on high will dawn upon us and visit [us] To shine upon and give light to those who sit in darkness and in the shadow of death, to direct and guide our feet in a straight line into the way of peace. [Isa 9:2.]

Psa.86:5 AMP
For You, O Lord, are good, and ready to forgive [our trespasses, sending them away, letting them go completely and forever]; and You are abundant in mercy and loving-kindness to all those who call upon You.

This denotes that forgiveness will bring peace to us and that God is good and is always ready to forgive.

We, likewise, should always be ready to bring forgiveness into any situation no matter how difficult it may seem, as this will instill peace to all parties involved in the conflict!

Matt 6:12, 14-15 AMP
And forgive us our debts, as we also have forgiven (left, remitted, and let go of the debts, and have given up resentment against) our debtors. For if you forgive people their trespasses [their reckless and willful sins, leaving them, letting them go, and giving up resentment], your heavenly Father will also forgive you. But if you do not forgive others their trespasses [their reckless and willful sins, leaving them, letting them go, and giving up resentment], neither will your Father forgive you your trespasses.

Mark 11:25-26 AMP
And whenever you stand praying, if you have anything against anyone, forgive him and let it drop (leave it, let it go), in order that your Father Who is in heaven may also forgive you your [own] failings and shortcomings and let them drop. 26 But if you do not forgive, neither will your Father in heaven forgive your failings and shortcomings.

God is very explicit in this scripture that unless we forgive, He is not in a position to forgive us! Those are very heavy instructions, and the reason that I believe forgiveness is one of the foundation stones for us to start building our life upon, once we have received Jesus (our cornerstone) as our Savior. It is VITAL that we forgive. I must stress that point over and over: it is a vital necessity! Our very life in Jesus can be polluted if we walk in unforgiveness and offense. Choose not to be offended and you will find it much easier to forgive. We can choose to forgive someone even when we cannot condone his or her actions! It is very important to separate the person from the action. Unless we make the distinction, it becomes an almost impossible task to forgive!

Matt 18:21-22 AMP

21 Then Peter came up to Him and said, Lord, how many times may my brother sin against me and I forgive him and let it go? [As many as] up to seven times? 22 Jesus answered him, I tell you, not up to seven times, but seventy times seven! [Gen 4:24.]

This scripture is taken from the example in Genesis 4:24, wherein Cain was in need of forgiveness seven times, but Methuselah's son (Enoch's grandson), Lamech (Gen. 5), had done many bad things and needed to be forgiven seventy times seven. That implies that there is no limit to the number of times we need to forgive. Just as it says in 1John 1:9, God puts no limit on His ability to forgive us as often as we ask. This does not give us a license to sin, but should we do so, He is always ready to forgive us.

1 John 1:9 AMP

If we [freely] admit that we have sinned and confess our sins, He is faithful and just (true to His own nature and promises) and will forgive our sins [dismiss our lawlessness] and [continuously] cleanse us from all unrighteousness [everything not in conformity to His will in purpose, thought, and action].

As you can see here in the scripture above, God is always ready to forgive us repeatedly. He knows our weaknesses and our shortcomings, as well as our sins (missing the mark). He has taken care of it all through the blood of Jesus. That is real gospel (good news)!

John 20:23 AMP
[Now having received the Holy Spirit, and being led and directed by Him] if you forgive the sins of anyone, they are forgiven; if you retain the sins of anyone, they are retained.

2 Cor. 2:10-11 AMP
If you forgive anyone anything, I too forgive that one; and what I have forgiven, if I have forgiven anything, has been for your sakes in the presence [and with the approval] of Christ (the Messiah), To keep Satan from getting the advantage over us; for we are not ignorant of his wiles and intentions.

Matt. 5:23-24 AMP
So if when you are offering your gift at the altar you there remember that your brother has any [grievance] against you, Leave your gift at the altar and go. First make peace with your brother, and then come back and present your gift.

To me, that means that God is not interested in our gifts unless they are presented with an obedient heart. Clearing the air can be so very beneficial for you and the other person. Even when you know in your heart that you have done nothing wrong, but the other person is holding something against you, be big enough and Godly enough to go to them and ask for forgiveness if they believe that you have wronged them in any way. It is not about who is right or who is wrong; it is about doing what our Father has instructed us to do, because He always knows best. This also keeps a direct pathway open to our Father through prayer!

Ps. 130:3-6 AMP
If You, Lord, should keep account of and treat [us according to our] sins, O Lord, who could stand? [Ps143:2; Rom 3:20; Gal 2:16.] But there is forgiveness with You [just what man needs], that You may be reverently feared and worshiped. [Deut 10:12.] I wait for expectantly wait, and in His word do I hope. I am looking and waiting for the Lord more than watchmen for the morning, I say, more than watchmen for the morning.

Ps 86:5 AMP
For You, O Lord, are good, and ready to forgive [our trespasses, sending them away, letting them go completely and forever]; and You are abundant in mercy and loving-kindness to all those who call upon You.

If God kept our sins on record, He would not answer any of our petitions; thankfully, He does not keep a record. He drops it when we repent and it is over. We are justified (just as if we had not sinned).

Our goal should be to follow God's example: always forgiving and let our offenses go, keeping ourselves pure before the Lord, so that our prayers will not be hindered. We also do not want to be a hindrance to those whom we need to forgive. Therefore we should not keep a record of things done to us, which give us opportunity to be offended. We also need to make sure that we are not taking on our friends' and loved ones' offenses. It is easy to become offended when we see those we love being maligned, and we need to be careful not to take the offense!

Recently I had an experience that really, really, required that I walk in forgiveness. I had a legal matter that was pretty much a slam-dunk, with a lot of written evidence, and what I needed to support my position. It was a mandatory arbitration matter; therefore it was up to the one person (the arbitrator) to decide the issue.

The opposing party's testimony was a total fabrication; however the individuals were not Christians, so I knew they were just doing what unsaved people do in such cases. There is no room for truth, only a means to an end. I had no problem with forgiving them. However, they called in people that I had been close to and those people supported the lies that were being told. I believed that it was because they walked in fear of their jobs. They were supposed to be Christians, so I needed special grace to walk in forgiveness with them.

I lost the case, not because there was insufficient evidence, but only because the arbitrator chose to believe the fabricated testimony, rather than the truth, and refused to look at most of my documentation.

I believe that sometimes God allows us to be in situations like these to show us how others can be hurt when Christians do not do the right thing. I knew that I had no choice but to forgive in order keep myself in right standing with Father God. Now this does not mean that I can trust those individuals in the future, but that has nothing to do with forgiveness. Reinstatement of trust can only come when there is repentance for wrong actions. I pray for all those people on a daily basis, including the Arbitration Judge handling the matter, as that is the only way I know to keep a pure heart with God. I would like to see them all saved!

You cannot be upset with someone if you are always praying for him or her and asking God to draw him or her to Himself, and turn that person in the right direction. I have always made an effort to deal that way with persons that have caused me harm. Unforgiveness can lead to bitterness, and not only do you hurt your spiritual walk when you don't forgive, but it can even affect your physical health. I have known several persons that have a lot of bitterness and unforgiveness suffering with severe arthritis. I am not saying that everyone who has arthritis is living in unforgiveness. However, healing can come to those that have this disease due to their unforgiveness and bitterness, usually as soon as they forgive and choose to walk in it.

Quite some time, after this case was over, I asked the Lord why He had allowed that loss and I was completely astounded by His answer: "it kept the door open for the salvation of the unsaved ones that you have prayed for so diligently over these many years."

What an eye-opener that was! God will always take care of us some way because we are His kids, but He is also concerned about the ones that have not accepted Him yet!

I now know that if they had lost the case it would have been a stumbling block to them, and God was more interested in their eternal salvation than in the case. Although I am still waiting to see the fruit of that harvest, I am certain it will come to pass and I still pray for them daily.

Unless we walk in forgiveness, we are unable to love as He tells us to love.

CHAPTER THREE

LOVE

I would like to share with you my experiences of God's love, and the love that He has for all of His children. He also has an abiding love for those that are yet to become His children! As you know, there are many different types of love, but I am going to leave the job of distinguishing of types for someone else to write about. I only want to share the agape love God has shown to me; He has instructed us to show that same love to the world around us. Our world starts in our own home, our own church and our own workplace. It then reaches its arms out to those all around us.

Remember how I told you when I first heard about Jesus as a wee girl? The love that came into my heart for this man, Jesus, was so overwhelming to me! I had never experienced anything like it! I simply fell in love with Him, yet I did not know where He was nor where He lived. I only knew I loved Him with all my being. This is the love the Father puts in our hearts when we have opened it up to the message of the Cross. It is something that cannot be explained by mere words. It is something that must be experienced. It is the love of God. I can't ever forget that experience and the love I felt that day! It is an experience that has stayed with me for a lifetime, and I love to recall it. It brings me great joy!

I have discovered that some people are easier to love than others. I am sure you have experienced the same thing! You know, the ones who are always trying to be an irritant to you and are not very loveable! It has always amazed me how God has this never-ending supply of love to give us regardless of the fact that we might be difficult to love at times. The Lord has also shown me that some folks need to be loved from a distance.

We can love people but we do not necessarily have to make them our bosom buddies! We do have a choice in the matter of friendship, but have no choice when it comes to loving. We do not need to put ourselves in the position of being tempted to take offense. That is why I say: sometimes it is better to love at a distance.

My favorite chapter of the Bible on love is the Amplified Bibles' version of 1 Corinthians 13. It is rich and so explicit about how we are to love! But first I want to share what God says about His love for us before I get into how we are to love others.

John 3:16 KJV
For God so loved the world, that he gave his Only begotten Son, that whosoever believeth in him should not perish, but has everlasting life.

This is the first verse I learned after I came to the Lord as a child. I think that is the case with many of us. It is the bedrock of our salvation. To think that God sent Jesus just for me - just for you! Those of us that have children can understand the implication of that act. Would you willingly give up your child to save a degenerate soul? I think not! Look at Abraham, whom God asked to give up his own son. The Word says that Abraham believed that God would raise him from the dead! Abraham had no proof of that, but he believed it, anyway. That explains why Abraham is called the "Father of the Faith." I wish that my faith would always kick in to that degree.

Heb. 11:19 AMP
For he reasoned that God was able to raise [him] up even from among the dead. Indeed in the sense that Isaac was figuratively dead [potentially sacrificed], he did [actually] receive him back from the dead.

Okay, I need to get back on track and stop going down a "rabbit trail" about Abraham. This is not about Abraham; it is about God's extreme love for us! This is extreme love!

1 John 4:7-12 AMP
Beloved, let us love one another, for love is (springs) from God; and he who loves [his fellowmen] is begotten (born) of God and is coming [progressively] to know and understand God [to perceive and recognize and get a better and clearer knowledge of Him]. He who does not love has not become acquainted with God [does not and never did know Him], for God is love. In this the love of God was made manifest (displayed) where we are concerned: in that God sent His Son, the only begotten or unique [Son], into the world so that we might live through Him. In this is love: not that we loved God, but that He loved us and sent His Son to be the propitiation (the atoning sacrifice) for our sins. Beloved, if God loved us so [very much], we also ought to love

one another. No man has at any time [yet] seen God. But if we love one another, God abides (lives and remains) in us and His love (that love which is essentially His) is brought to completion (to its full maturity, runs its full course, is perfected) in us!

1 John 4:16-21 AMP
And we know (understand, recognize, are conscious of, by observation and by experience) and believe (adhere to and put faith in and rely on) the love God cherishes for us. God is love, and he who dwells and continues in love dwells and continues in God, and God dwells and continues in him. In this [union and communion with Him] love is brought to completion and attains perfection with us, that we may have confidence for the day of judgment [with assurance and boldness to face Him], because as He is, so are we in this world. There is no fear in love [dread does not exist], but full-grown (complete, perfect) love turns fear out of doors and expels every trace of terror! For fear brings with it the thought of punishment, and [so] he who is afraid has not reached the full maturity of love [is not yet grown into love's complete perfection]. We love Him, because He first loved us. If anyone says, I love God, and hates (detests, abominates) his brother [in Christ], he is a liar; for he who does not love his brother, whom he has seen, cannot love God, Whom he has not seen.   And this command (charge, order, injunction) we have from Him: that he who loves God shall love his brother [believer] also.

    These scriptures do not require a lot of explaining. It is what God said and God means just what He says. Had God not loved us first, we would not be able to love. We all have unsaved friends that are quick to say they love us, but how can they really when they do not understand what love is? Without God's love in us, we are unable to love unconditionally. We have to really work at trying to love some people, but God finds it so easy because He Is Love. God does not just have love in Him; He is entirely made up of love. It is His very being! He cannot be separated from it. Although we are not made of love, we can be so filled with His love that it exudes from us. We are made in His image; therefore we should show His qualities.

I have known true love in my life, for which I am very grateful. My husband, my children and certain close friends all have loved me unconditionally. That is how God meant it to be. My first-born, Zoe Leeta, grew up surrounded by love. Although she had a few setbacks along the way, she was always a happy person. I always said that it would never occur to her that there might be someone out there who did not like her. She just took it for granted that everyone truly liked her! She loved people and people loved her. Even during her long, seven-year battle with cancer, she always kept a happy spirit. I can just see her laughing with Jesus: up where she is experiencing all the love that He has for us!

How am I to love others? How do I show that love? Let us examine what God said about the subject! Keep in mind that God put nothing in the Scripture that we are unable to accomplish. If we find it in the Word, we can do it! Look closely at this passage of Scripture:

1 Cor. 13:1-8a AMP

If I [can] speak in the tongues of men and [even] of angels, but have not love (that reasoning, intentional, spiritual devotion such as is inspired by God's love for and in us), I am only a noisy gong or a clanging cymbal. 2 And if I have prophetic powers (the gift of interpreting the divine will and purpose), and understand all the secret truths and mysteries and possess all knowledge, and if I have [sufficient] faith so that I can remove mountains, but have not love (God's love in me) I am nothing (a useless nobody). 3 Even if I dole out all that I have [to the poor in providing] food, and if I surrender my body to be burned or in order that I may glory, but have not love (God's love in me), I gain nothing. 4 Love endures long and is patient and kind; love never is envious nor boils over with jealousy, is not boastful or vainglorious, does not display itself haughtily. 5 It is not conceited (arrogant and inflated with pride); it is not rude (unmannerly) and does not act unbecomingly. Love (God's love in us) does not insist on its own rights or its own way, for it is not self-seeking; it is not touchy or fretful or resentful; it takes no account of the evil done to it [it pays no attention to a suffered wrong]. 6 It does not rejoice at injustice and unrighteousness, but rejoices when right and truth prevail. 7 Love bears up under anything and everything that comes, is ever ready to believe the best of every person, its hopes are fadeless under all circumstances, and it endures everything [without weakening]. 8 Love never fails [never fades out or becomes obsolete or comes to an end]

I love this portion of scripture. God has made it so clear to us how His love in us is supposed to be released to those around us. When we hear an evil report about someone, do we just believe it, or do we give him or her the benefit of the doubt? It says we are supposed to believe the very best of every person. The reason so many rumors run rampant is because the Body of Christ does not put that scripture into operation. We should not be talebearers, and our hopes are not to get sidetracked, so that we can believe the very best of everyone. If the tales are supposedly founded on truth, then we should pray for the person to repent and get back in fellowship with God. Prayer and repentance are very powerful forces. But talk to God about it, not all of our acquaintances! If we talk to God about all of these issues, it will quiet the rumor mill. The thing about a bad rumor is that even if it is proved to be wrong, people still remember it. Words cannot be taken back once they are in the atmosphere. Words are so important!

We should always have loving words and good reports. God framed the world with His Words, thus we should frame our world with our words. If we do not like what we have in our world, we should check out our transmission of words and see what we have been putting into the atmosphere. If you have bad confessions out there, repent and retract them, and get back on the path! We are not to keep score of the things done or said to us or about us. God's love in us does not insist on having its own way. We are willing to let the other person have their way, as God evens it all out in the end!

Can you imagine the kind of world we can build for ourselves if we just employ the instructions God has given us about our behavior? We can be "blessed and highly favored" in this life, if we keep the rules God has set out for us to follow! We will build a wonderful world for ourselves when our foundation is God's Word.

I do not recall a time that I ever doubted God's love for me. Even during the hard times of my life, I always knew that He loved me. Just last year, a lot of people were getting gold teeth as a supernatural sign from God when they asked Him for it. I never asked God for a gold tooth, because I did not really think about it. I have all of my teeth, so it was not an issue. But as I was brushing my teeth, lo and behold: there was a gold tooth! I said "Lord, why did you give me a gold tooth? I didn't even

ask for it!" His reply was amazing: "just to say I love you!"
Now how special is that? God is truly a God of Love!
I am here to tell you that father God loves you
just as much as He loves me! He is no respecter of persons. Knowing the love of God does not always come
overnight. We need to walk with Him and have an inti-
mate relationship with Him. I know that He loves me
because He has shown it time and time again. He is
forever faithful! I can truly say with the Apostle Paul:

Rom 8:38-39 AMP
*For I am persuaded beyond doubt (am sure) that neither death
nor life, nor angels nor principalities, nor things impending and
threatening nor things to come, nor powers, 39 Nor height nor
depth, nor anything else in all creation will be able to separate us
from the love of God which is in Christ Jesus our Lord.*

**Obedience, Forgiveness and Love open the door for
God's richest blessings.**

CHAPTER FOUR

HEALING

1 Peter 2:23-24 NIV
When they hurled their insults at him, He did not retal-
iate; when he suffered, He made no threats.   In-
stead, He entrusted Himself to Him who judges justly. 24 He
himself bore our sins in His body on the tree, so that we
might die to sins and live for righteousness; by His wounds
you have been healed.

I like to paraphrase this and make it personal to
me each day: "I entrust myself to the One who judges justly, by Whose stripes I was healed."

Healing has been one of my core beliefs for
practically all of my Christian life. Had it not been for
the healing hand of God, I would not be here today.
We tend to remember those incidents in our lives that
are of a spiritual nature and we have them imbedded
in our "memory bank," so to speak, to make a
lasting impression on our lives. I wrote about some of
these instances in my introduction, but I want to reiter-
ate some of them again.

The earliest of them is from when I was an infant. My sister tells me that I was around five months old. I remember being in the back bedroom of a little home with my mother and we were both very ill and bedfast. I was lying in my mother's arms. You would think the room would be dark, but it was very light to me, even though the blinds were closed. I could always see her there with me. That is my first memory and I know that if it were not for the hand of God I would not have survived scarlet fever, without damage, at that young age. I praise God that both my mother and I got well.

Again, when I was four years old, I was riding with my father. I was asleep in the back seat of our car. None of the cars had seat belts in those days and when another driver struck us head-on, it threw me through the windshield of our car. I still have a scar on the top of my head where the glass cut me. I remember the horror of that night. A young boy in the other car was trapped under the seat of his father's car and his drunken father kept sitting on him, even though we were trying to get him out.

That incident is also imbedded into my "memory bank" and I can recall it just as you would a movie I remember us standing out on the highway by the cars. There was real frenzy on the highway that night with crying, swearing and blood; yet I remained calm. I know that it was only a miracle of God that the only injury I sustained was the cut rather than a concussion or other complications. It was an unpleasant scene, but I was not afraid! I was more concerned about the little boy in the other car than I was about myself. For a four year old to react in that manner, It could only have been the hand of God on me that night! As you recall, I mentioned earlier about laying hands on Mama Potter when she would get sick with headaches and other symptoms associated with early menopause. At the time I had no idea what the cause was, but I did know that if I laid hands on her and prayed, Jesus would take her pain away and she would be well! This happened time after time! I really did not know to pray for the cause to be eliminated; I just prayed for the pain to go away. I cannot express enough the importance of teaching people how to pray for the sick. Jesus answered my prayers and used the gift he put in my hands, but I did have to develop it over the years, as He taught me the value of learning how to pray and how to build up faith for the healing. I am also thankful for the gift of faith, which I will cover later. I did somewhat recognize the gift of healing He had put in my hands and I talked with Him a lot about the subject.

My favorite memories of my communion time with God, as a young girl close to ten years old, was when I would go down to the creek alone. I would sit on the grass and sing my heart out to the Lord. I made up all my own words, and accompanied myself on an old worn out guitar that only had 3 strings left on it, which I did not know how to play, but I played with all my might! It was just me and Jesus and it did not matter what the sound was like; only birds, and some squirrels now and then, were listening. It was only what my heart was feeling for Him that mattered to me. It brings tears to my eyes even now, as I recall how precious it was!

Isn't it a wonderful thing that age is never of relevance when we are talking or singing to Jesus? I can do the same thing today and it brings the same joy to my heart!

It brings joy to the heart of the Savior, as well. We are always His children, regardless of age!

Earlier I shared with you the open vision I had of hearing the voice of the Lord speak after I had shot the devil and he had to leave my room. I believe it was just prior to the time of the open vision that the Lord placed the gift of healing in my hands. It has always remained there. I had shared that vision with Mama and Daddy Potter and they in turn shared with our Pastors. Everyone was excited that little Lois Lee was called to preach! God did not say that I was called to preach in that vision, and I believe many times people can misinterpret what God means when He speaks to someone else. They were well-intentioned people, just not discerning. Mama Potter never pressured me to become a preacher, however.

The word "preach" simply means to "tell" and there are many ways of doing that other than behind the pulpit. Perhaps she knew that. We never talked about it much after that. Looking back, it is so much easier to see what God had in mind when He spoke to me than it was in 1942. I have gone into all of the world in so many ways, yet never in the conventional "missionary" way. However, God anointed me to be able to use the finances He blessed me with to do His work through others who were called for that purpose.

My pulpit turned out to be the boardroom and I wish that youth could be taught that the Kingdom of God is made up of many areas, and we can be called to any one of them.

Being a minister for the Lord is not limited to the Church. We are to be His ministers wherever He places us. Had anyone told me in 1942 that mine would be the

58

business world, I probably could not have understood that either. In my business "pulpit," I have been asked many, many times to pray for the physical healing of people. The world of business brings with it a platform all its own. You can use your platform any way you choose.

I used mine to deliver prayers for the ones who asked. Many were from the Sales Manager of the last dealership I worked for who called me on the phone to state, "We need some prayer power, Mom." When you get to be a certain age, you kind of become "mom" to everyone! My daughter, KJ, also experienced requests time and again. People in the world know whom to call when they have a special need.

I married at the age of 16 and started my family early. My oldest child was born just eleven months later in May of 1950: a beautiful baby girl.

My husband, Bill, developed Tuberculosis early in our marriage and we believed it to be because of his military service, since he was in the Navy during WWII. The VA gave him all of his hospital and education benefits, but no pension benefits. He had been hospitalized on two prior occasions, one of which resulted in a large portion of one lung being removed. That was in 1953-54.

At that time we had two children, a handsome son had been born in March of 1953. Bill's surgery took place in Albuquerque, New Mexico; so Mama Potter cared for my babies to enable me to be with my husband. He was discharged from the hospital in 1954 and we went to Denver as his family now resided there.

Bill was attempting to regain his strength so he could pursue a career in accounting, which was his major during his two years in college. I went to work for a small manufacturing company that made the first rubber plugs to fix flat tires on automobiles. I did well there and was made supervisor. When I left, the Corporate Accountant gave me a letter of recommendation and he put it on his company letterhead. I mention this because it had a purpose in God's plan, although I did not realize it at the time. God used it when He had me apply for the Office Manager's position.

During those years I did not have much opportunity to use the gifts God had already placed within me, but I did not realize that He was not finished with the endowment of His gifts.

Bill became ill again in 1958. We had moved to Oklahoma City and back to Denver again during those years, so we were living in Colorado at the time he became ill. He was admitted to the Veterans Hospital in Denver. The Tubercular ward was on the fifth floor of the hospital and the children were not allowed to go up to see him. (We had three children at this time, as our youngest child, a beautiful baby girl, had been born in Oklahoma City in 1957.) I was working in Denver when Bill was hospitalized and was able to support our children, but it was a very difficult time, as they could only wave to their father from the grounds below the window.

After about a year of hospitalization he was not getting any better. The doctors reported that the hemorrhaging from his lung was getting worse and only surgery would correct it. Although he had only a 10 percent chance to make it through the operation, they scheduled him for immediate surgery.

Our relatives and friends had all been praying for him of course, but while I was visiting him the night before surgery I was led to lay hands on him and speak healing to his body. As I laid my hands on him I knew in my spirit that he was healed. I just knew that I knew that I knew he was healed! I asked him to request new x-rays the next morning before he went to surgery, which he did. They took the new x-rays, but found no evidence of the hole that had been in the lung and the hemorrhaging had ceased. They were perplexed and decided to keep him in Denver for a few more months, then decided to transfer him to California to a facility that was better for recuperation. It also allowed the children to visit him on the grounds.

After he was transferred, I moved to California. I got a job immediately, which was another miracle of God, and after three months I brought our children to California. Bill came home from the hospital after about two years. I believe it was 1962. They had finally decided he had no further signs of tuberculosis. Bill has had no recurrence of that disease to this day! Jesus had performed a creative miracle that day in Denver!

But God...has a plan

Luke 17:12-19 KJV
And as he entered into a certain village, there met him
ten men that were lepers, which stood afar off: 13 And
they lifted up their voices, and said, Jesus, Master, have mercy
on us. 14 And when he saw them, he said unto them, Go
shew yourselves unto the priests. And it came to pass, that, as
they went, they were cleansed. 15 And one of them, when
he saw that he was healed, turned back, and with a loud
voice glorified God, 16 And fell down on his face at his feet,
giving him thanks: and he was a Samaritan.17 And Jesus

*answering said, Were there not ten cleansed? But where
are the nine? 18 There are not found that returned to
give glory to God, save this stranger. 19 And he said unto him, Arise, go thy way: thy faith hath made thee whole.*

That scripture denotes to me a creative miracle for
the one that came back and gave thanks. I believe the nine
were made clean of their leprosy, but the last
one was made WHOLE! I believe that the ears, hands, toes,
or whatever parts had been eaten away by this insidi-
ous disease, were all restored. I believe they were rec-
reated or, if you will, made whole! Praise Jesus! That was
a creative miracle.

I had witnessed healings, but when Bill was healed
in 1959, that was the first actual creative miracle that
God had performed for my eyes to see the result!

This chapter on healing is so intertwined with faith
that it is almost impossible to separate the two. The words
of our mouths are so connected to our faith that they can
hardly be separated. Therefore, I'm combining faith and
words into one chapter. Many of my experiences
have some of each in them. The gifts of the Holy Spirit
work together.

My life had been so hectic and in such turmoil over
the years, that my Doctor had me on a tranquilizer, named
Librium. I also suffered from serious migraine headaches
and the medication slowed them down a little. I was 21
years old when I started taking Librium and the only time
that I did not take it was when I was pregnant with
KJ.

I had some surgeries, which also helped, but
finally the stress of working, raising a family, and all
that comes with the issues of life caught up with me.

This happened in 1965 when we were rear-ended by a car and my eight-year-old baby girl was injured with a deep gash on her head. The accident caused great trauma for me even after I was told she would be okay.

I did not know why I was feeling so sick and had no energy, so I went to my doctor. He referred me to another doctor that admitted me to the hospital. Before I knew what was happening, I was put on all kinds of drugs and I was placed in a psychiatric hospital. They said that the accident had been the "straw that broke the camel's back" and that I was having a nervous breakdown. The new doctor had not told me what he was treating me for at the time he admitted me to the hospital.

I had started back to work during this time. My Because of all the drugs they put me on, I did not have the will in me to fight back against the darkness that had invaded me. I sat and stared at the wall, in a complete catatonic state. By the time I would barely become myself again, it was time for more medication. I always knew that if they had just told me what was happening I could have fought against it, because I was a born fighter and stubborn to a fault when I needed to be. I had not even been warned! I was hospitalized for several months and then they started giving me electric shock treatments.doctor felt working would help me. I had lost my original job, but found another quite quickly.

A lovely woman named Ann, who was thirty years my senior, worked in my new office. She loved working for me, but understood my memory problem, since the treatments wiped out my short-term memory and I could not remember where my books were located from one week to the next - bad situation for a boss! I never forgot how to do my work, just where everything was kept!

Once she realized the problem, she began to promptly bring me all my books and everything I needed, placing them on my desk. She was an angel.

She worked for me at other dealerships after that. And we remained friends for the rest of her years on earth. I had a "Precious Promises" box on my nightstand, and would read one each night, but had a problem remembering the long verses if I had not previously memorized them. One night I pulled Romans 8:31. It just said, *"If God be for us, who can be against us?"* I made it a point to speak that verse every day, saying it over and over again!

Although I was home from the hospital, I was still going in for the electric shock treatments and was on medication. I was on 400 mg of Thorazine per day while in the hospital, plus several tablets of Librium in addition to nine grams of Tuanal per night for sleep. I do not know how I was able to function at all! As I recall, they had started weaning me off the Thorazine to come home, but kept me on the full dosage of Librium and Tuanal. Librium was a drug similar to Valium, and was being widely used at that time. Of course the shock treatments wiped my short-term memory, so it was a bad situation.

One evening everyone in the household had gone to some function and I was home alone. I got ready for bed and took my usual meds. A little later I thought, "Oh, I forgot to take my meds," and took them again. A little later the same thing happened. When they found me I had overdosed and I was rushed to the hospital.

When I awakened the next morning, I was in the lock-down ward. I had never been in there before. Apparently, they put me there because they were not sure at that time if the overdose was accidental or not. There was a woman in the "cell" next to me and she tried to reassure me by saying, "Oh, honey, don't worry about it, I've been in and out of here for 10 years and you'll get used to it." My spirit rose up within me and I got that determination which quickly turned to an anger that was strong for a person of my mild disposition. I knew I could never get used to that and this would be my last time!

I demanded to see my doctor. It was only seven o'clock in the morning and they said he would not be in until nine o'clock! I demanded to see him the minute he came in. They assured me that they would advise him. My righteous anger burned within me for those two hours!

When nine o'clock came they led me from lock-up to the doctor's office. I marched in with my head held high in defiance. He asked me to take a seat. I told him I could say what I had to say standing up. I searched my memory for the most awful word I could think of to use to describe what I wanted to say and, since I had never used curse words, I said the only bad word that came to mind. I looked at him and said, "I am no longer going to come to you for treatment of any kind and I am never going to take another one of your damned pills! I want out of here and I want out of here right now!" He looked at me in great surprise, but he could tell I meant business.

He told me that I could not just quit taking the medication all at once as I had been on it for so long. He informed me that I would have to stop it gradually or I would get very ill, to which I replied: "You just watch me!"

I left there that day and I threw out all of my medication. Now, please, I am not advocating that you throw out your medication! I am just telling you this personal experience of how God worked in me. I kept going to work and I felt wonderful. In about three weeks the same doctor personally called me one morning and asked if I would stop by. I reminded him what I had said about never coming back to see him. He said, "Well, not for an office visit, but just to say hello." I agreed and stopped by on my way to work. He looked at me with a very surprised expression and said, "Hello, you look well," to which I replied that I felt wonderful and I left. I knew that he had expected me to be in extreme withdrawals from the medication by that time, but did God have a surprise for him! God had completely healed and delivered me. I never suffered from one single withdrawal symptom, praise Jesus! The Lord restored all of the brain cells that had been destroyed by the shock treatments and my excellent memory was completely restored to me. *"If God be for us, who can be against us?"*

I never saw that doctor again, but I did pray for him for many years that he would come to know Jesus, as he had been an agnostic. I feel certain he has passed by now, but I trust that he was ready.

Joel 2:25-27 KJV
And I will restore to you the years that the locust hath eaten, the cankerworm, and the caterpiller, and the palmerworm, my great army which I sent among you. 26 And ye shall eat in plenty, and be satisfied, and praise the name of the Lord your God that hath dealt wondrously with you: and My people shall never be ashamed. 27 And ye shall know that I am in the midst of Israel, and that I am the Lord your God, and none else: and My people shall never be ashamed....

The person that I had been that was so insecure and could never stand up for herself had suddenly become a new person. I now had a boldness that surprised even me, as I had never experienced it before. I was not only healed, but I was changed! I was no longer the emotional wreck of a person that I had been. I had a new identity in Christ! He was now the only one I needed to look to for my self- worth. My worth was in Jesus and He had paid a high price for me!

Some years later, when I had become more mature in God, I asked Him how I had allowed myself to have this breakdown. He reminded me that at one point I had requested the Holy Spirit to please not manifest Himself in me at a certain church I was attending. They did not believe in speaking in tongues and I was concerned that I might offend someone. Out of my ignorance concerning how the Holy Spirit operates, I had opened the door for the enemy to wreak havoc in my life. "Quench not the Spirit" is in the Bible for a reason!

1 Thes. 5:19-21 AMP
Do not quench (suppress or subdue) the [Holy] Spirit; 20 Do not spurn the gifts and utterances of the prophets [do not depreciate prophetic revelations nor despise inspired instruction, exhortation, or warning]. 21 But test and prove all things [until you can recognize] what is good; [to that] hold fast.

Thank God, that we can all learn from our experiences, and when we inquire of Him where we missed it, He will tell us.

I have found that many of the times I have experienced dramatic healings since then, were when I became very angry at the devil. Not angry with

67

God nor a person, but at the enemy and the circumstances that I knew were not what God wanted for me. Those were the times when I received healing manifestations: when I said, "enough is enough; I am not going to put up with this anymore! I will no longer tolerate what the enemy is doing to me!" Those healings I received by standing on my own faith, separate from the ones where others have laid hands on me, or when God had given me a sovereign touch.

Since I am focusing on healing in this section, I will fast-forward to approximately 1979. The Rev. Joe Jordan was ministering at the Holiday Inn in Torrance, California for Full Gospel Business Men's Fellowship International (FGBMFI). He was known as "God's chiropractor." He called for people that needed healing for backs, etc., and I went forward.

My body went into the most unusual contortions you can imagine when he laid hands on me. I was in positions I would never have been able to do on my own. I accepted and received my healing.

However, as an added bonus, God healed me of hypoglycemia, which was very extreme in me. I had suffered from it for years and on occasion had actually lost consciousness when my blood sugar dropped.

Diabetes was prevalent in both my mother and father's families and I had been advised that I would also likely have it. Hypoglycemia is usually a precursor to diabetes. My youngest sister had juvenile diabetes type one and had been on insulin since the age of two. I had given up all sweets and was literally on a diabetic diet. I had not been able to skip meals at all. God healed me that night.

About three weeks later, we got up a little late on a Sunday morning so I had decided to skip breakfast, which was not unusual for me since my healing, and off to church we went.

When we pulled up in front of the church, every single symptom of hypoglycemia hit me. I broke out in a cold sweat with a terrible headache, sick to my stomach, feeling like I was going to pass out. Rey took one look at me and knew I was in trouble! He asked, "Do you want me to take you home?" I shook my head "no" and, at that moment, my spirit man rose up within me and I said loudly, "satan, in the name of Jesus, I was healed and I will not allow these false symptoms back into my body!" Instantly, every symptom left my body and I was completely normal. Those symptoms have never returned.

A few weeks ago I had a blood test for diabetes at my doctor's request for a physical examination. It was completely normal, as I had told him it would be. Praise the name of Jesus! Get mad at the devil! It is okay to vent your anger at the enemy, the devil, who only wants to kill, steal from us, and destroy us.

Hollywood Presbyterian held services called "Life In The Spirit" on Friday evenings at the time Dr. Lloyd Ogilvie was Pastor. They invited different spirit-filled speakers to come in and hold the meetings that were held in Wylie Chapel rather than the main sanctuary. We had gone to several of those meetings and God was moving mightily.

In the fall of 1984, Rey and I had been asked to come and do three consecutive Friday evening meetings. It was the last Friday of our series and Rey was ministering in the healing line at the end of the service. I usually ministered alongside him, but on this particular night I was seated in the second row, praying silently. The Lord spoke to me. He asked me to go to the microphone and announce that someone was there that needed a healing in their kidneys and if they would come forward, He would heal them. I did not respond immediately, so He spoke to me again. I did not respond, because I felt I would be interfering with the prayer line, but the third time He spoke it was very commanding and I responded at once!

I spoke out what God had instructed and waited. A woman in the back came forward and I took her to one side and there prayed with her. I first prayed for her to be filled with the Holy Spirit, as God led me to do, and then for her healing. God had said if the person would come forward, He would heal her kidneys. I did not even ask her what her problem was because the Lord already knew what she needed. I never doubted for a minute, because God always keeps His Word! We prayed and cried together, and she also knew that God was faithful to His Word! I had not seen her at the meetings before and I did not even get her name.

About a year later I was standing in my bedroom and this incident came to my mind. I told the Lord I would sure like to hear a report on the woman that had been healed that night last year. I then went about whatever I was doing and didn't think about the matter anymore. About 10 minutes later my phone rang. It was the man that handled the scheduling of the meetings for Life in the Spirit. He was inquiring if we could come back and hold another three sessions for them. I told him that I would ask Rey to check his schedule and get back to him.

He then asked, "Guess who I sat next to at a banquet last Saturday night?" Of course I said I didn't know, so he said, "I sat next to Kaye S." (name abbreviated for privacy), to which I replied, "and who is Kaye S.?" He said, "Oh, you know, the lady you prayed for last year that got the healing of her kidneys!"

He then went on to tell me of her remarkable miracle and that he wanted her to come and give the testimony when we came back to hold the next meetings, if we would like her to. Of course we wanted her to come! That was a really fast answer to my prayer and I do not even know why I would be surprised at that, because God has usually been very swift to answer!

Kaye had been a missionary who was forced to come home due to her kidney problem. She was born with congenital defects of the kidneys, which over the years had caused deterioration, and she had been scheduled to go in to start dialysis. She was of the persuasion that miracles had ceased with the last apostle. However, she heard while attending BelAir Presbyterian that God was doing miracles at Hollywood Presbyterian, and she had come to check it out. She knew she was healed that night, so did not go back to her doctor for dialysis.

A few months later she had gone back on a non-kidney related matter and her doctor insisted on doing a scan of her kidneys. He was shocked to find she had two new kidneys! God is still in the business of doing creative miracles!

God also taught me something through that experience. I had always felt that I could not be used fully since I do not have a real "dynamic" delivery when I speak. I tend to be more soft-spoken than many of my lady friends in ministry. Yet, part of Kaye's testimony was that my soft-spoken way was what drew her. God then told me that He made me that way for a purpose!

Another beautiful thing happened on our second ministry session at Life in the Spirit. A lovely senior woman that was a member of the congregation
attended the healing service. That was very unusual, as
most of the people attending were not the "pillars" of
the main church, but were drop-ins. I was surprised to
see her there, but it soon became evident why she had
come when she approached me and asked how she
could have faith for healing.

The Lord gave me an immediate answer for
her. Are you born again? I asked her, to which she
replied, "Oh, yes!" I explained that the same faith she used
to become born again is the faith she uses to obtain her
healing. I could almost see the light bulb go on over her
head, as she understood for the first time what it meant to
have faith to believe God for healing! We then prayed together for her healing, in faith believing! It was a wonderful experience.

As many times as I have witnessed healing
miracles, I've also wondered about all the bad things
that may have been avoided because of the grace of God. I
am thinking about the time in 1982 when we were
driving home from our dealership in Huntington Beach
and were in Torrance going toward our home in Palos
Verdes. Suddenly we were rear-ended by another car. It
struck us so hard that my glasses flew off my face into
the back seat of our car. We pulled off the street rather
than block the traffic on busy Hawthorne Boulevard. We
pulled into the customer lot of a department store that had
already closed for the evening. The other car pulled in be-
side us. The woman driving the other car asked if we
were hurt and Rey replied, "No, praise the Lord, we are
not." She said, "Oh, you are Christians." It turned out she

was also a believer, so we held hands and prayed together, thanking Jesus that there were no injuries.

We became acquaintances and saw her several times at church after that. We encouraged one another in the Lord. She was a local banker and had worked late and was really tired that evening, which had prevented her from being able to stop in time. She had insurance to cover herself and all was well.

That was only one of the times God spared His people. There have been many more and probably a lot more than I can even imagine! I am sure I have kept my angels really busy looking after me all these years!

I remember in 1982 when we were attending a service in which Pastor Ed DuFresne was ministering. Pastor Ed has a unique healing anointing. He does not always look at the individual he is praying for, but literally sees into their bodies. He approached me and started praying; then he told me that the Lord was cleaning out all of my veins and arteries. It only lasted for a few moments. He declared that they were all cleaned. I received the Word of the Lord and the healing that was spoken over me.

A few years went by and I was diagnosed as having atrial fibrillation. My cardiologist did a conversion to bring my heart back into normal rhythm, but it only lasted about 10 days then went back into irregularity. My Doctor said he wanted to do a cardio- lite test to check all of my arteries. I advised him that they were all clear and I had no build up in my system. He stated he wanted to check it anyway, so I said it was okay if he wanted to verify that they were clear.

He put me in outpatient at the hospital, pumped the blue dye through my body, and when he was finished he stated, "Well, all of your veins and arteries are completely clean." I knew that when God does a thing, it is done well! Praise God for His faithfulness!

My precious husband, Rey, went home to be with Jesus on October 6, 2003 and my precious oldest daughter, Zoe Leeta, went home to be with Jesus on February 13, 2005. I thought that I adjusted pretty well after Rey went home. Considering his condition he did not suffer long, for which I was very grateful. Within 30 days of the beginning of treatments, he had gone to his reward. It just seemed like the Lord had me in a bubble and I was really protected from a heavy spirit of grief.

It seemed harder when my daughter passed. She had suffered for seven long years and although I was grateful she was not in pain anymore, it just did not feel right. It is not natural for a child to precede the parent and it was difficult. I had lost my joy.

By this time my rotator cuffs had gotten so bad that I could not even raise my arms over my head, only bend them at the elbows, during praise and worship. I could no longer sleep on my side, as I had so much pain in my shoulders. I was not well and was admitted to the hospital twice at the end of May, 2005. My medications were just not working well and had thrown my chemical balance out of whack!

I recall vividly the night of June 3, 2005 and I had just been home from the hospital for a couple days, and was still very sick, although I had gone to church that Friday night. I was extremely weak and could not sleep. It was getting close to midnight and I was standing in my bathroom. I got so angry at the devil, I really started telling him off, that I had taken all I was going to take, and that I was not going to tolerate anymore.

At Integrity Christian Center that evening, Pastor Kenny Gatlin preached on not tolerating anything from the devil. He said sometimes we just tolerate things. We tend to think that unless it is something life- threatening, we just have to put up with it! He told us that we are not to tolerate anything from the devil. It really struck home with me. I realized that I had been tolerating a lot, and I refused to do it anymore.

I went to bed just before midnight on June 3, 2005 and fell asleep immediately! When I awakened at 5 a..m. on the morning of June 4, 2005, I knew at once that there was a difference in my body. I had a sense of wellbeing throughout. I jumped out of bed. I threw my arms in the air and started dancing around my room.   My joy had returned. Overnight, He had turned my mourning into joy! It was bubbling over. I was healed.

My daughter, KJ, came running upstairs from her bedroom, wondering what was going on, as she had been very concerned about me and thought something was wrong. Did she have a surprise in store! I was dancing up and down the hall.

When she realized that I was healed, we were dancing up and down the hall together; it was a joyous time! My rotator cuffs had been completely healed, as my arms that I could not raise over my head were stretched toward Heaven, praising the Lord! I was filled with energy, whereas before I had just been dragging myself around. God had visited me in the night hours between midnight and 5 a.m. and completely rejuvenated my body!

I wanted to call everybody and tell them, but it was so early. Being considerate I did not, although I could hardly stand to wait! Later, Pastor Kenny said he would not have minded me calling him at 5 a.m. on a Saturday morning to tell him of my miracle healing. You see, those rotator cuffs had been bad for quite a few years. I do not really remember how long they had been in that condition. I had just been tolerating it! My visits to the hospital never disclosed why I had severe dizziness, but God had healed that, too.

As soon as it was 8 a.m. in Texas, I called my sister! As soon as it was 9 a.m. in California, I started calling: Pastors Kenny and Brenda Gatlin, Dr. Bill and Barbara Peters, my son Ray Alan, my son-in-law Jerry, my daughter (Rey's daughter) Irene in Palm Springs, and the list went on and on. I was so overjoyed that I could not keep it to myself! I do not remember if my daughter KJ called anyone or not, but we were dancing and shouting and praising God all over the house! We serve such a mighty God! It gives Him great pleasure to heal and deliver His children! He is so good!

There are so many times that God has met me for needs in my body that I cannot possibly record them all here, but I am certain that before this book is finished there will be more testimonies of healings I could record, because God is still healing on a daily basis. I pray for others each time the opportunity presents itself. Our God is forever faithful.

But God...has a plan!

CHAPTER FIVE

FAITH AND WORDS OF OUR MOUTH

I have found that our faith and the words of our mouth are very closely intertwined. It is almost an impossibility to separate them. Our words either build up our faith or tear down our faith and get us into unbelief. That is why I am combining them into one section. When we are standing firm in our faith, our words will help us maintain our position. If we are wavering in our faith, it is usually because we have been speaking words of doubt or unbelief and they have undermined our faith. Fear is an archenemy of faith. The word of God keeps our faith strong and enables us to please our Father.

Rom 10:17 NKJV
So then faith comes by hearing, and hearing by the word of God.

Heb 11:1 NKJV
Now faith is the substance of things hoped for, the evidence of things not seen.

Heb 11:6 NKJV
But without faith it is impossible to please Him, for he
who comes to God must believe that He is, and that He is a re-
warder of those who diligently seek Him.

As important as faith is in our walk with the Lord, so are the words of our mouth. We see over and over how people plant their seeds of faith, and then dig them up again by the words they allow to pass their lips. There have been many times I have prayed for an "instant crop failure" for words of unbelief. We must train ourselves as to how we should speak. I have tried to train myself to do what I refer to as "measuring my words." I make a habit out of thinking about what I am going to say before I say it.

Some people misinterpret this at times, thinking I am without words, however I am just "measuring" them to see if they line up, before I allow them out of my mouth. That was something that took a lot of practice – a lifetime as a matter of fact. I do this in the business world as well as the church world or the home environment. All of these arenas are important in our lives. They all produce a harvest and we need to make sure they produce the type of harvest we had intended to produce in our lives. It can waste a lot of time to have to re-till the soil and replant. Sometimes there is not the opportunity to do so, and we miss out on God's best! We really need to try to get it right!

Rom. 4:17 NKJV
(as it is written, "I have made you a father of many
nations") in the presence of Him whom he believed

*God, who gives life to the dead and calls those things which
do not exist as though they did;*

Prov. 18:21 AMP
*Death and life are in the power of the tongue, and they who in-
dulge in it shall eat the fruit of it [for death or life].*

Matt. 12:36-37 NIV
*But I tell you that men will have to give account on
the Day of Judgment for every careless word they have spoken.
37 For by your words you will be acquitted, and by your words
you will be condemned."*

I am so thankful that confessing Jesus as Lord acquits us, aren't you?

Since the Lord started using me in the gift of healing at such a young age, it came quite natural that I understood the workings of faith. Now that does not mean that I was always able to implement it, but I did understand it. I was able to extend it as it applied to healing. I then had to learn how to use that faith in other areas of life.

I must say, however, that knowing how it operated for healing did make it easier to implement in other situations. I had learned how to trust God! I thank God for starting me out early. It is an ongoing exercise and a constant work in us. We are all truly works in progress.

Learning to measure my words proved to be a little less of a challenge; even though I had never been taught that the principle of life and death is in our words. I had, however, practiced this from a young age out of necessity. Although, looking back, I can see times that God had the control of my mouth. His doing that for me paved my way and made it much easier. I am sure you can remember similar times in your own life.

I had my first little job when I was seven years old. I was living with a married cousin who lived next door to an older woman that lived alone. The woman paid me 15 cents every Saturday to bring in her daily paper and pick up her groceries from the market. It paid for a movie and a soda, and I was so thrilled with my first job! This was my first experience with money management. Of course I was not with my cousin very long before I moved to my next home, but my job was great while it lasted! I had acquired a small measure of responsibility.

Learning to watch and measure my words was a way of life for me, although I did not understand the principle. It has lasted a lifetime, but like everything else, it requires constant practice. I discovered quite young that my mouth could get me in a heap of trouble, and that keeping my mouth shut could keep a roof over my head and food in my tummy! That was really important from five to nine years old. However, there were times that I spoke that I came to realize as an adult those words had not been chosen by me. They had to have been words ordained by the Holy Spirit.

An example of this was the day I met Mrs. Potter. I was at her mother's house playing with her younger sisters, who were my age. She was the oldest of 13 children, so there was a large span of years between oldest and youngest. We met and she asked me if I would like to accompany her downtown. Being a small town, it was only a few blocks to "downtown." I said sure. Since I was on my own, I didn't even have to get permission from anyone.

We were walking along and she was holding my hand. It was the spring of 1942. I was nine years old. I looked up into her face and very innocently stated matter of factly, "I would sure like to have you for a mama." Somehow, they found my father and got his permission for the Potters to take me to live with them. I never left their home until the day I got married. The bond we had forged lasted throughout their lifetime. I was always their daughter.

Now this was not a pre-planned speech, just a statement from the heart of a little girl that recognized a loving heart that was ready to share it with her. I only learned recently, while listening to a tape of an interview with Mama, that she had concerns about taking me with her to town that day. She said in the tape that she wanted me so badly that she was afraid she might kidnap me! That day was indeed a divine appointment! It was all God.

That day changed the course of my life! There were many times over the years that God just gave me the words that I spoke and I was as surprised as anyone was as to what came out of my mouth! Don't you absolutely love those moments?

When God downloaded the accounting ability into me in January 1956 at age twenty-three, He also gave me the managerial ability I needed. I was in charge of all the office personnel, as well as the service cashiers, who worked in the shop. I was able to get along with most people and that served me well. I had practiced getting along with others since I was a small child, as I had lived in all those different homes between the ages of five to nine.

I was very sensitive to people as well as things in the spirit realm. As I have said, the likelihood of my staying in a home was better if I got along with others, so it was an art I had practiced. The only home I felt secure in was with Mama and Daddy Potter. They were the only ones I had ever called Mama and Daddy, except for my birth parents.

Anyway, this gift also served me in the business world, and when I went to work in the office environment; it was a real plus factor. The original owner, a wonderful man, sold the dealership after a year and a half and the new owners kept on staff. It was a partnership, and the two men who owned it were of opposite personalities.

They brought in a new Service Manager who was of a "high roller" type. That did not set well with me, as it went against my principles. God had taught me the business, and it did not include "creative" accounting. (That was of questionable ethics.) He was writing up phony repair tickets under warranty. I did not book them, as there were not proper offsets in accounting, and I was not going to create them!

The owner that I usually tried to avoid came into my office one day and asked about the repair tickets. I told him they were not booked. He wanted to know why. My usual shyness evaporated and I became very bold. I said, "Because I know how to keep an honest set of books, but I do not know how to keep a crooked set of books." He said he was instructing me to book those tickets! There was a huge double stack of them on my desk and I picked them up with both hands. I said, "If you want these booked, you can do it yourself!" And I threw them at him! Repair orders flew everywhere, as the stack was monumental. He stood there with his mouth open, unable to speak! I picked up my purse and walked out without looking back!

Afterward I realized I had just quit my job! That was one of the times the Spirit of God rose up in me and I spoke out with no thought of what I was going to say. The times that I do not measure my words and they just come out of me spontaneously, I always know it is God speaking directly through me! He is giving me the words that I am to speak.

We felt it was the will of God for us to move back to Colorado at that time, so we sold our house. Bill gave notice on his job and we moved. Little did we know that in less than a year, Bill would be back in the hospital and Colorado was a better place to be for his health, due to the climate.

But God…has a plan

It is amazing how that when we start remembering instances in our lives when we have heard from God, we think of the little things that only He can bring to our recollection. When I was a freshman in high school and I was taking Algebra, I did not enjoy it at all. I loved Math, but I did not like Algebra. It just did not make any practical sense to me, yet I could look at the problems and my head would just come up with the solution. I did not work them out; I just somehow knew the answer. I always aced my tests, because the answers made sense, but not the equations. Looking back, I believe God was giving me another "download" just as He did with accounting later on, when I needed it. I do not know why, I just understand that He did that for me. So many things He has done for me have been simply because He loves me!

Another instance when He filled my mouth was when I had my first job after arriving in California. I had my choice of two jobs upon arriving in Los Angeles. One paid slightly more than the other did, but I took the advice of a man working in the office at Motor Car Dealers Association as to which dealership he thought would be the best fit for me. He was a kindly gentleman, whom I considered an older man. He was probably only in his late fifties, but to a twenty-seven-year-old, he seemed like an older man! It sounds funny to me now when I recall it! So even though the pay was slightly less, I took the job at the dealership he recommended.

The position was filling in for the Business Manager who was on sick leave. After I got there, I found out that she had cancer, was very ill, and was not expected to return. It just was not discussed. While I was waiting to be able to bring my children out, I rented an apartment that was quite close to her, in Los Angeles, and visited her often. After about three months, I moved to Glendale and brought my children out from Denver.

God had really prepared me for this position, as the dealership that I had worked for in Denver was a large operation. We had around fifteen women in the accounting department alone, and it was a fast- paced office. The Comptroller was a brilliant woman, but she had a real problem relating to people. She wanted the work done, but did not have the patience to train anyone how to do what she wanted done. The turnover was incredible! The month-end pressure was so great that girls would just quit due to her sharp tongue when she was impatient.

She observed that the women would sneak around and come to me for help when they did not know how to do a task. Although it was not part of my job, I would always help them. After all, God had taught me how to do it all and it came so easy for me! Of course I couldn't say that, so the Lord just let me look like I was really smart! He told me that He would let me take the credit if I always gave Him the glory! Because she observed this, and saw how well it was working, she came to me and asked if I would take the position of her assistant and train the girls at their desks, as she just didn't have the time nor patience for it herself. Of course I accepted, as it was a promotion for me!

We became great friends after that and I learned about factory-owned dealerships from her. I believe she learned a lot of people skills from me as well. I even visited her at her home after I moved to California when I would go on vacation to Denver. I would pray for her, as I could tell she was unhappy despite the fact that she had comfortable surroundings and a good job. The pressure of her position was tremendous! Without the Holy Spirit working daily, the car business can be brutal! The Holy Spirit was my secret weapon!

When it was determined that the position I had at the dealership in California would become permanent, another woman in the office wanted the job. She did not have the ability or qualifications, but wanted the position based on her tenure. I recall so vividly the day the owner called me into his office and posed the question to me. He asked if I would be willing to train her for the position and then work for her, since she felt she should have the position. The words that came out of my mouth were in no way related to the emotions I was feeling on the inside. I had just brought my children to California and I really needed this job!

But I said, "No, Sir, I could not do that. I would never be able to work for someone that I did not respect for knowing more about the business than I do. However, if you want to put her in the position, I will understand. I have only been here for a short time and she has been here for a few years. I will be able to find another job".

He thanked me and said he would make a decision and get back to me. I thanked him for his time and left his office. I had peace as I drove home that night. I knew I would also be out of a car, as I was furnished a company vehicle! "Way to go, Lois," was my unvoiced thought. But I knew those were not my words that came out of my mouth in the owner's office that day, so I had peace and was totally calm!

The next day, he called me in and told me that he had decided to give me the position of Business Manager. He said that when he talked to her she had been extremely emotional and was crying. Yet, when he talked to me, I had been calm and controlled. He felt those were the qualities he needed in a Business Manager. Praise God for His Holy Spirit! I had a wonderful working relationship with that owner for as long as he lived. When he passed away a few years later, it was almost like losing a father; that was the kind of relationship we had forged.

I was only twenty-seven years old at the time I took the job and all of the women in my office were older, but I had a good relationship with them. It is so important to listen to the Holy Spirit and let Him speak through you. It can be life or death. It can be prosperity or lack. It is up to us!

It was a few months after Rey came into the Kingdom of God and we had gone to Walteria Assembly where we were attending services at the time. It was New Year's Eve and Rey was being baptized in water. We were leaving the parking lot around midnight to go to our home in Palos Verdes and Rey was joking that it was sure unusual to be dipped in water on New Year's Eve instead of drinking scotch and water; all we had to do was make it home and not encounter any drunks on the road. I said, "Well, the Lord has His hand on us." At that very moment I saw our daughter KJ out of the corner of my eye as she was leaving the parking lot in her little Corvette and said, "And He has His hand on Karla also." KJ was on her way to Pasadena to meet her cousins at the Rose Bowl to camp out overnight and watch the parade the next morning.

The next morning around five o'clock when Rey went out to the kitchen, KJ was there. She was visibly upset, trembling all over. Of course he was concerned and asked her what was wrong, as she was supposed to be in Pasadena. She related what had happened.

As she was driving to Pasadena, traffic was quite heavy going through the tunnels on the Harbor Freeway. The one-way tunnel was several lanes wide and she was in the far left lane. The car to her right suddenly swerved in front of her and hit the side of the tunnel, causing it to flip. The driver hit the pavement in front of her. She slammed on her brakes to avoid hitting the body on the pavement. KJ is, without a doubt, the best driver I know, but that situation was not in the hands of the driver.

When she slammed on her brakes, her car turned

completely around so that it was facing the oncoming traffic. She could hear the squealing of tires and sound of metal crunching all around her as the cars started running into each other and piling up. The police were soon on the scene. She had not hit the person on the pavement, but his crash and being thrown from his car had taken his life.

Eight cars had been involved in the pile-up because of the accident. KJ's hands were so gripped to the steering wheel she could hardly pry them off. She was in a state of shock. Her car was untouched, even though it had spun around in the wrong direction, facing all of that on-coming traffic. Not one car had touched her! The Officer commented, "Someone up there must really like you. Do you need me to drive you out of the tunnel?" She decided to drive herself and return home rather than going on to Pasadena and the overnight campout for the parade.

God indeed had His hand on her that night! God used that incident to, once again, show me the power of the words of our mouths.

Another example of the power of words is the time we had gone to my daughter Zoe Leeta's home to accompany her to my grandson John's graduation. She lived in a beautiful two-story home with a large staircase that had a marble landing. It led to the upper bedrooms. I was on the upper floor and everyone else had already gone downstairs. As I stood at the top, I felt an extremely strong shove against my back and I started to tumble down the stairs. I was going head over heels. All I could say was "Jesus!" as I hit from one side of the doublewide staircase to the other in my tumble.

When I came to the bottom I landed on my head on the marble! I got up and without thinking, I started praying in the Spirit with a voice of authority, and I was touching my body all over as I prayed. My family came running, as they thought one of the children must have fallen for Gram to be praying that loud and serious! But, no, it was Gram herself that had fallen!

I had a knot on my forehead, but that was the only visible injury. Not a one of my long fingernails was broken! They wanted me to go get myself checked out, but the Gift of Faith had risen up in me and I was sure that I was not injured!

We proceeded to go to the large University Stadium where the graduation ceremony was to be held. It was packed and the only parking was a long way from the seating. My son-in-law stopped the car to let me out near the bleachers, but I refused to get out. I was so mad at the devil, I was going to walk every step of the way just to spite him! Any other time I would have been happy to save the walk, but not that night! I walked the full distance of that stadium parking lot and then all the way to the top bleachers! I know it was the Gift of Faith that had fueled me, because I am not an athletic person. That's a fact to which anyone who knows me can attest. I laid hands and some ice on the lump on my forehead and the swelling disappeared. I never had any repercussions from that fall! God is good!

I have heard it asked, which of the gifts in 1 Corinthians 12 is the most important; and the answer remains the same, "the one we need at the moment!" At that moment, for me, it was the Gift of Faith backed up by the words of my mouth!

One of the scriptures given specifically to me by Brother Dick Mills in May 1983 is:

1 Cor. 12:9-10 KJV
To another faith by the same Spirit; to another the gifts of healing by the same Spirit; 10 To another the working of miracles; to another prophecy; to another discerning of spirits; to another divers kinds of tongues; to another the interpretation of tongues:

I praise God for all the gifts of the Holy Spirit that are available to us to do His work and carry out His will on the earth. I treasure His Gifts.

But God...has a plan

CHAPTER SIX

TITHING, GIVING AND RECEIVING AND PROSPERITY

One of the things I learned from Mama and Daddy Potter was tithing. They were always tithers as well as givers. From the eyes of the world they had little, but I know they were wealthy people in the Kingdom. No matter how little they had, they always gave God His ten percent and more; yet we never had need of shelter, food or clothing. We always had gas in the little Model T and, later, the Model A that was our transportation to church. Mama could cook the best meals in the world. She was also an excellent seamstress, and I was always well dressed. No one knew that many of my clothes were made from used clothing, which had been given to her. She had taken them apart and used the good material to make me "new" clothes! She could just look at a picture and then duplicate the dress. Mama was extremely gifted.

Daddy worked in the fields, mostly cotton fields. I had a choice: I could help Mama with housework or I could work with Daddy in the fields. I chose to work with

Daddy in the fields most of the time, although I was required to learn housework as well.

I enjoyed working with Daddy in the cotton field. When it was time to "chop" cotton, he got me my own little hoe. It was much smaller, and easy for a nine or ten year old to handle. I knew nothing of farming, so on my first day I just started hoeing away.

Daddy looked back and my row was clean as a whistle! Uh-Oh! That began my first lesson about "chopping" cotton. It meant to chop the weeds out of the cotton plants, while leaving the cotton plants intact. I was literally chopping the cotton: weeds, cotton plants and all! Daddy did not get upset with me, but patiently explained the process. He had the same patience when it came time to pull and/or pick the cotton. Pulling meant boll and all, while picking meant you picked the cotton from the boll. Both processes were used, depending on how the farmer wanted it harvested for the cotton gin. We mostly pulled the cotton which required gloves be worn, as the bolls had sharp edges.

After I was married, when Bill was attending the university in a neighboring town, I pulled cotton for the season to bring in extra money. The Kansas City Star did a series on how veteran's wives were helping their husbands through college. They came out and took pictures. A picture of me pulling cotton, with my cotton sack over my shoulder, was published in the Kansas City Star. My precious father-in-law was so proud of that picture that he carried it in his wallet. It was still there when he went home to be with Jesus in 1955.

I have always been grateful that I was taught good work ethics and was never afraid of hard work! I did not know then that the Bible says if you don't work you don't eat, but by then I already had the work habits!

All the money I earned, I tithed on. It was just understood; the first ten percent belonged to God. It was really easy for me, since I had the gift of giving deposited into me those years before in that little church when I had first heard about the man: Jesus of Nazareth. I fell so much in love with Him that Sunday that I, as a little bit of a girl, gave Him every penny I had in my pocket! The love for giving and the joy of giving has never left me!   I believe that when we truly fall in love with Jesus, we will truly want to give our all to Him.

People used to ask me what I was doing for my retirement plan. I never really thought about it, because Rey and I gave all that came into our hands. I would just reply, "Well, God is our retirement plan." I was much younger then, but our plan never changed. Of course, that strategy may not be for everyone. It was just where we were in our walk with God. Each of us has our own destiny to fulfill.

Now I am retirement age, and I am depending on God for my every need. I know He is faithful! As David said, "I have never seen the righteous forsaken, nor their seed out begging for bread." There were many times over the years that God asked us to prove His faithfulness. Those are some of the things that I will so enjoy sharing! Running with God is an exciting marathon indeed!

I did not see any spectacular miracles in my early years, as far as money was concerned, as I did in the latter half of my life, but the everyday faithfulness of God is every bit a miracle! He usually always provided for me by way of a job or two - as a means of taking care of my family and me. I was never without a job. I worked at whatever I could find to do. I worked as a nurse in the hospital in my youth, and then was a waitress for a few years at different coffee shops. I would work nights in a nursing home after working all day at the Tyron factory.

Many times I worked two jobs at the same time, because it was necessary. When I went to Albuquerque to be with Bill while he had surgery, I worked as a waitress in a coffee shop and also as a maid in a motel. God always had jobs for me to do, and I never considered any job too menial for me! That was God's provision in those early years. In 1956 when the Holy Spirit trained me for the car business, I knew I had found my niche and that is where I stayed. It paid well compared to other work and, since God was my instructor, I did the job well and gained a good reputation in the industry.

With the upbringing I had from Mama and Daddy Potter, it never occurred to me to apply for government assistance to help me with my babies. By then I had learned that the Bible said if you don't work you don't eat and that was all I knew! God always provided. I am not saying it is wrong to get assistance; it was just not the way God provided for me.

Bill was a hard worker when he was able to work, and after his release from the hospital our life became easier financially. He went to work in the automobile business as well but, unlike me, he hated the industry. I loved it! He wanted to return to Kansas and the family farm, which by then had oil wells to tend. We divorced and I asked for nothing, because it was the right thing to do. I started all over again from scratch, just God and me!

It is amazing how miracles can start happening when two walk in agreement. After Rey and I were married, I believed God for his salvation for Seven and a half years and then it happened. Rey had previously walked away from a bad marriage, took nothing and was starting from scratch as well. Therefore, it was just God, Rey and me! In the meantime, God was working miracles in the business realm.

We were in the recreational vehicle business when almost all the dealers were going broke due to the energy crisis. God provided a special moneymaking way for us with our bank and we had all of our needs met. The bank was getting back an enormous amount of repossessions and they asked us if we would keep them on our lot, recondition them at the bank's expense, and then sell them for the bank.

So while others were locking their doors and going out of business, God was providing a way for us to meet our payroll and other expenses. We had great favor with our bank and after the recession at that time was over, we received a letter from the Vice President of the bank in San Francisco commending us for how we handled our obligations while others were defaulting. We had never interacted with him, but somehow he had become aware of us. That meant a lot to us, because we had given glory to God.

Rey recognized that it was the favor of God, even though he had not yet had an experience with Him at that time. Rey was raised Catholic and knew about Jesus, but had no relationship with Him. I knew that it was because we had been sowing seed into the Kingdom of God, as Isaac did during the famine in the land. That was the same year we had opened our second RV lot, and our grand opening fell on the day of the oil embargo in the mid-1970s. Oh, we serve a God who is forever faithful, even during famine!

In early 1978, we had purchased a co-op in Redondo Beach that was right on the Esplanade. Our unit was one of the penthouses on the beach side and we had a marvelous view. We were rarely there, as we spent most of our time in our home in Palos Verdes. When our daughter Zoe Leeta got married, she and her husband had lived in the building for about a year and the building owners made it available to be purchased by whoever was leasing. Jerry and Zoe Leeta didn't want to buy it because she was pregnant by that time and the building did not take children.

As Rey and I were also on the lease, we decided to take advantage of the offer to buy the unit. We started looking for a home in Manhattan Beach that would be suitable for them, as they wanted to remain close to the beach. While Zoe Leeta and I were driving through Manhattan Beach in June 1978, we saw a man posting a for sale sign outside his home. We stopped and looked at it. Although the house was small, the location was excellent. I put a deposit on the house to take it off the market until Rey could look at it.

Rey immediately saw the possibilities of a complete remodel, which would make it into a three bedroom, two-story home. We explored the idea with the planning commission and found out that it could be done, so we entered into a sale agreement. The sellers were very pleased, although the next-door neighbor was not at all pleased. He had wanted to buy the home if it ever went on the market. We were there at the exact moment the sign was being put up, so we got the home! I knew I was at the right place at the right time: God's time! We entered escrow at what we considered a good price.

That July 4th weekend, when we wound up at FGBMFI and God started a string of miracles in Rey's life, never ceases to amaze me. At the men's luncheon they were requesting all of the men to give $4,000 to complete the new World Head-quarters building in Costa Mesa. Although Rey did not totally understand it all at the time, he felt it was the thing to do. It was a real step of faith, as we were really stretched financially, with the new home purchase in es-crow. We were just recovering from the second energy crunch and Rey thought, "Really? Four grand!" But he stepped up and did his part! He knew I would be in agreement with him as I always was, and I knew this was God working in Rey.

Well that very afternoon, Rey received a phone call from Zoe Leeta telling him the sellers of the property had called her and said they had found an-other house and needed to close escrow early. They said if we would agree to close early, they would reduce the price of the house by not $3,000, not $5,000, but you guessed it…$4,000! That really got Rey's attention! It was yet another miracle of that special weekend!

So, after the kids moved out of the Redondo Beach property, we furnished it to our taste. It was two bedrooms, one of which was a loft. You could just lie there and listen to the ocean. It was beautiful. Unfortunately we didn't really have time away from work to stay there often, so we stayed in our Palos Verdes home. The beach home became a vacation place for ministers and friends that needed time away to rest.

Rey would just stock up the refrigerator and invite them to stay for a week or two. They would have complete use of the unit and privacy to enjoy their stay. Rey even made sure there were quarters in the jar just in case they needed to do laundry. He never forgot anything! It was a source of joy to us to be able to bless God's people. Rey also had the gift of giving.

In the mid 1980's, when we felt we were to sell the Redondo Beach house, we got an offer much lower than the unit was worth. After praying about it, God said to Rey, "Let it go; I take care of my own." So we sold it. God had already told us the profit was to go to a certain person in town that we knew.

We knew he was going through a difficult time in his life, but didn't know details of his situation. We just knew that God wanted the proceeds to go to him, not to us. That was one of the reasons we had hesitated to take the low offer. But God spoke that we were to accept it. When the sale closed we took the check and did not even deposit it in our bank, but instead took it to this minister and just endorsed it over to him in its entirety. Although it was not a huge amount, he later told us it was just the exact amount he needed desperately at that time.

But God...has a plan

When it came time to renew our dealers' license with DMV in 1979, the insurance companies refused to issue bonds to any of the dealers without an enormous premium being paid, because of all the dealers that had gone out of business.

Therefore, even though we had never defaulted or had a claim against our bond, it was just a business decision on their part. It was a justified decision, as they had paid a lot of claims against the defunct dealers. This meant we would have to post a cash bond with the DMV, or pay an exorbitant amount of $2,500 instead of the usual $100 to the Insurance Company for the bond, and that was a yearly premium. A cash bond would be $5,000 cash to the DMV. Wow! That was a blow! We did not have $5,000 cash lying around! Without a DMV license, you're out of business! We started praying and calling on our Lord.

That very afternoon we received a letter from Rey's mother with a cashier's check for $5,000. We never discussed business or finances with Rey's mother, who lived very modestly in East Los Angeles. It would have taken her a very long time to save up $5,000. She just felt she should send us the money!

She, though a devout Catholic, had not understood being born again until I had led her in the salvation prayer and Rey saw to it that she was also baptized in the Holy Spirit. So she now found it phenomenal that, in her older age, she could actually hear from God and get her prayers answered. It was through prayer that she had heard from God to send her son $5,000 as a gift.

Isa 65:24 NIV

Before they call I will answer; while they are still speaking I will hear

Of course, we thought immediately that our need had been met for our dealer bond. The Lord spoke to me and said, "Send it to Oral." I said, "Lord, this was a gift to Rey from his Mother, so if you want it to go to Oral, you're going to have to tell Rey that!" (We had been partners with Oral Roberts Ministry since before Rey became born again, and had continued to partner with that ministry.)

I just kept the check in my purse waiting on instructions. It didn't take long. In a couple of days Rey came to me and said, "Loi, I believe God is saying to give the $5,000 to Oral". I just smiled and said that yes, I was hearing that, too.

Rey got on the phone with our local representative from Oral Roberts Ministries, a wonderful man of God. While speaking with him on the phone, they set up a breakfast meeting for Monday morning. We decided to just endorse over the cashier's check, as it was.

We met the following Monday morning and handed him the endorsed check. He questioned us if we were certain that was what we wanted to do. We assured him it was. He then told us he would be meeting with Oral on Thursday and would personally sow it at that time, for the need we would specify. He then asked us to tell him of the most important need we had. Almost in unison we said, "For our daughter KJ."

She had been in a serious accident with her Corvette and it had been practically totaled. She had spent time in the hospital. Her physical injuries were not as bad as her emotional injuries. She had been blamed for the accident, although it was not her fault. The occupants of the other vehicle, a van, had switched places in their vehicle, as the actual driver had been drinking.

Their explanation of the accident was an erroneous shifting of blame. The injustice of it all upset KJ greatly.

At that time, she was struggling with the concept of being baptized in the Holy Spirit with evidence of speaking in other tongues. She had been attending a church and a school that did not hold with that belief, yet she saw the fruit of it in others' lives. We wanted her to be healed emotionally and to be at peace with her new beliefs. That was what came out of our spirits at that breakfast meeting. The $5,000 was planted for her spirit, soul and body. No thought or mention of the DMV bond ever came up.

Now let us fast forward to the following Thursday. It started pretty much like any other day at the office. Suddenly, in the early afternoon, KJ came bounding through the door, jumped up in the air, and clicked her heels together. Now that would not seem so spectacular for her except that her back had been so bad she could hardly walk. Her face was aglow; what a testimony she had.

She had been spending the week at the beach, as she was trying to recuperate after returning home from the hospital. While sitting in the sand on the beach, reading her Bible, she was singing to the Lord. Suddenly she started singing in another language! Startled, she looked around to see who might be there. There was only one man, sitting in a beach chair reading the paper. He dropped his paper below his eyes, looked at her, and smiled, as if to say: "That's okay."

She started singing again and the same thing happened. Her heavenly language came forth and she looked up. The man was gone. She could see a good quarter of a mile each way on the beach and he was nowhere to be seen!

She gathered her Bible, towel and whatever else she had and ran to the condo, taking the steps two or three at a time, to the top (fourth) floor. She was not taking the elevator on that occasion! She was healed! The seed we had planted that was delivered to Tulsa that same Thursday had indeed brought forth fruit!

The next day, I got a call from my Insurance Agent saying that he had a call from the Insurance Company. They said that they had decided to cover our bond for the standard $100 premium although, at that time, the minimum premium was no less than fifty percent or $2,500. He said, "I don't know what happened; it just came out of the blue!" Well, we knew what had happened: God had intervened in our affairs! Obedience in our finances had brought forth swift rewards!

Later, when our daughter was recalling these events to her friend, the mother of the young girl who was a passenger in her car the night of the accident, she had another surprise. The mother said, "That description of the man on the beach is the same as the man that was at the scene of the accident! He was very tall, blond and bronzed, just as you described. He had looked at me and said, 'I guess you know why these girls were saved here tonight, don't you?,' after he had seen the Ichthus (fish) shaped window on my van. I turned back to speak to him and he was gone!" KJ has never had any doubts about having seen her angel!

That particular instance of sowing seed was not just a return in finances, but also something much better. Our daughters' healing and personal experience with the

Holy Spirit that she will never forget was a far better return than money! Not every seed you plant is necessarily for financial blessings, but you cannot put a price tag on the change in a life! The financial blessing we received was just a bonus that God threw into the package!

But God...has a plan

We had closed the new location in Van Nuys, California we had opened the day of the oil embargo. However, we had taken an option to purchase the property there. We had exercised that option, even though we had closed the business. It was not an easy decision, as we had to continue making mortgage payments. We knew the property could be sold for much more than we were paying for it, so we had exercised the option. This decision was prior to Rey's conversion and I know this was just God imparting His wisdom into the matter.

In 1979, we went to the FGBMFI World Convention in New Orleans. It was a wonderful convention and it was there that we met Sir Lionel Luckhoo, who was also a new Christian and he and Rey had become very close. Their close friendship lasted the rest of their lives here and I know continues in heaven.

While at the convention, the Fellowship was asking for an offering from the men for the needs of the Fellowship. They were asking the men to give $5,000 each. Rey felt the Lord telling him to give $10,000. He talked to me about it, and I said we needed to do what God was asking us to do. That was a real sacrifice for us, as it was a time when interest rates were at an all time high! We had the property in Van Nuys up for sale but, with interest at over twenty percent, the market was just not moving. To give $10,000 would put us in a real vulnerable position, but God asked us to do it, so that settled the question. We gave the offering unto the Lord. The convention was wonderful and God was really moving among the people.

We had a real surprise when we got home! The realtor called and said he had a buyer for the commercial property in Van Nuys. It didn't matter that interest rates were over twenty percent, because God had found us a cash buyer that wanted to build a strip mall on the property. What a blessing! We gave God the $10,000 offering and he sold our million-dollar property immediately - to a cash buyer, no less! God had proved His faithfulness once again!

We thought we could just put the money in a safe investment, live off the interest, and retire for a while! Sounded like a good plan, but God had different ideas! He wanted us to buy an automobile dealership in Huntington Beach, California. So, there we were, in 1980, off to a new adventure with God! I believe it was the only car dealership in Southern California that had a chapel. We saw God move in mighty ways over the two years we had the dealership. Many lives were changed: lives of our customers as well as the lives of our employees. There were remarkable miracles that occurred in both our lives. It was a tremendous time of spiritual growth for us in many areas.

I would like to share one or more remarkable incidents that occurred because of our obedience to the Lord in opening that dealership.

We had a young man in our employ by the name of

Kelly. He worked in our service department as a lot person. He always seemed reliable; although we were aware he had problems at home with his parents. One day we had a call from our local police department telling us that one of our vehicles had been in an accident. The vehicle was an inventory unit and was not supposed to be off the lot, so we were very surprised. They said the little truck had been totaled, although the driver, Kelly, was not injured.

This was a problem, as Kelly had taken the vehicle without permission, which, according to our company rules, meant he had in fact stolen the vehicle. That meant a mandatory termination of his employment.

I felt bad about it, because I liked Kelly a lot. Of course, he did not come back to work, as he knew the consequences. I requested payroll to prepare his final check and requested our service manager to call him and ask that he return his company uniforms and pick up his check, which the manager did. I also told him that when Kelly came in to pick it up, I wished to speak with him.

Rey was still a new Christian at the time, only two years old in the Lord, and just was not prepared to deal with this situation. He did not want to see Kelly, no way, no how!

When Kelly came into the dealership, I took him into the chapel. He was very humble and apologetic about the accident. I explained to him that was not what I wanted to talk to him about. I then proceeded to share with him about Jesus. He was a very troubled young man whose parents were not together and neither parent wanted Kelly to live with them, even though he was still in his teens at the time. He was living with another family and felt misplaced.

I prayed with Kelly and he then stated his desire to accept Jesus into his heart. We prayed together, and he received the Lord. I knew that with all the spiritual warfare in his life he really needed to be baptized in the Holy Spirit. I presented this to him and he was very open to receiving. I told him I was going to get Rey to come and pray with him. He said, "Oh, no, he won't want to see me!" I assured him that was not the case, but that Rey would be most happy to come and pray with him. I was speaking in faith and knew that God would have to work a miracle in Rey's heart as well.

I went into Rey's office and told him I needed him to go minister to Kelly. His response was, "Oh, no, you minister to him." I told him he had just become born again and it was important for him to lead Kelly into the baptism of the Holy Spirit. He didn't want to but after thinking about it for a few seconds, he realized it was the right thing to do, the God thing to do. So he got up from behind his desk, marched into the chapel, and proceeded to hug Kelly, welcoming him into the family of God. Then he led him into the baptism of the Holy Spirit, with the evidence of speaking in other tongues. It was a glorious time. He then asked Kelly if he would like to work at R Family Dodge. Kelly was of course happy to say yes.

Rey called our service manager on the phone and told him that he had a young man in his office named Kelly that he wanted to hire, and asked him if he would get all the proper applications for employment. Our manager was flabbergasted and said, "Boss, you just had me fire him!" Rey said, "No, that was the old kid, Kelly. This Kelly is the new creation in Christ that we are now hiring!" It was a day of rejoicing indeed!

The following Saturday night we had a FGBMFI meeting and Kelly came. Guess whom he brought as his guest? Our service manager! When the invitation was given at the end of the meeting, Kelly accompanied the service manager to the front to accept the Lord! What a joy that was for us all! God had taken a situation that the devil meant for evil and had turned it into good. We serve such a good God! Through it all, we had also grown in the Lord, understanding more of His ways.

The money we invested in R Family Dodge was not returned to us in dollars, but it was certainly returned to us in souls, signs, wonders, and miracles! Word went out among the car dealers that Rey Soto had a chapel in the dealership and to many that seemed almost unbelievable! Rey was well known in the industry for several years before he came to Christ and having a chapel was not what they thought of when they thought of Rey. He was a tough, honest, no-nonsense businessman. The word traveled fast! Some people visited the dealership just to be prayed for by us.

Another rewarding incident was when a man who was in advertising, which Rey had known for many years, came in to see Rey. I had done advertising with his son as well, and thought the man had retired as he was now in his eighties. He and Rey caught up on old times and of course, Rey shared with him that he had become born again. He did not understand what "born again" meant. Now, this man had taught Sunday school in his well-known denominational church for over twenty years, but no one had ever shared the born again experience with him. Amazing, isn't it? We all just presume that everyone in the church knows these things. Rey took him straight to the book of John.

John 3:3-7 KJV
Jesus answered and said unto him, Verily, verily, I say
unto thee, Except a man be born again, he cannot see the king-
dom of God. 4 Nicodemus saith unto him, How can a man be
born when he is old? Can he enter the second time into his
mother's womb, and be born? 5 Jesus answered, Verily, verily, I
say unto thee, except a man be born of water and of the Spirit,
he cannot enter into the kingdom of God. 6 That which is
born of the flesh is flesh; and that which is born of the
Spirit is spirit. 7`Marvel not that I said unto thee, ye must
be born again.

After Rey had gone through the scriptures with the gentleman, he said he wanted to be born again as well. Rey led him in the salvation prayer, and he truly became born again and knew it!

Of course, Rey never left it at that. He immediately took him into the scriptures that were about the baptism in the Holy Spirit and, in no time at all, he was speaking in an unknown tongue. It was unknown to us, but known to God. What a glorious day that was, indeed! He said, "I have been missing this my whole life and did not even know about it!" He was one joyful person!

There were so many instances of God "showing up", and "showing out" His power. There was never any doubt about why He had wanted us to invest the money He had given us into that dealership. It was not for us to make a lot of money, although there is nothing wrong with making lots of money, but He had a higher purpose! Those were probably the roughest two years I have ever seen in the car business, but a glorious time in the Kingdom!

It was winter of 1981 and I was sitting at my desk with one of our bankers. He looked at me and said, "Why do you guys keep going here when business is so lousy? You could have just retired and not have all the headaches that the business brings these days. Why do you do it?"

I looked at him, and although my insides were screaming out, "You are so right," I replied very calmly, "We are doing this because God asked us to do it. We will be here until He says different". His only answer to that was, "Well, I guess that's a good reason!"

After he left I said, "Lord I really need a Word from you right now. I am hurting! Things are going badly! Money is so tight! Taxes are due! You always provide, I know. You have never failed us, but I really need a Word from you right now! Talk to me!" He did. He simply said, "Jeremiah 29:11." I swung around to my credenza, grabbed the little NIV Bible that I kept there, which is still my favorite, and went immediately to Jeremiah 29:11. Up until then, I did not have that verse in my memory bank and was totally unfamiliar with it. I was overjoyed when I read it.

Believe me, since then that verse has never left my memory. It became rhema to me that day! When a scripture goes from logos to rhema, it is a marvelous experience. God has given me several verses like that and they become seared in your heart! That day it was, "For I know the plans I have for you, declares the Lord, plans to prosper you and not to harm you, plans for a hope and a future." I just wrote that out of my memory bank!

Jer. 29:11 NIV
For I know the plans I have for you," declares the Lord, "plans to prosper you and not to harm you, plans to give you hope and a future.

I did not have it perfectly, but the meat was all there, thank you Jesus! It was the little precious moments when I had a special word from God that became so very pertinent over the years.

Those are experiences t h a t n o man, woman or devil can rob you of, because you know that you know that you know, you have heard from God! That was how the two years at R Family Dodge were spent.

We did not go away totally empty handed, though we certainly did not go with anywhere close to the million we had when it all started. However, we did leave knowing that we had obeyed God and He was well pleased!

The year was 1982. We were selling R Family Dodge. The buyer that God told us to accept was a well-known automobile dealer. Our books were in perfect order and I insisted that the only way we would sell was for them to buy out the corporation's stock, which was ten years old at that time. We had utilized the name of our RV dealership, just giving it a new DBA.

It is very rare for someone to buy the stock of an active corporation. I would never buy someone else's ongoing corporation. It is hard to know what you are getting without extensive audits and could still be subject to undisclosed liabilities. The customary way is to buy certain assets, only. I knew we did not need accounts receivable, and all the other corporate attachments, hanging around our necks to distract us. I really felt God saying that was the way He wanted it done. I knew that only God could impress them to accept those terms.

As unbelievable as it seemed, they agreed! Because our sales tax audits had been so good for all our years in business, the auditor came out, stayed less than an hour, signed off on our returns, and waived the other years, so we were done. Their auditor was there for part of a day and he was done. All of our due diligence over the years had paid off, and God used it for His glory. Prosperity comes in different ways!

I like the phrase I learned from Dr. Bill Peters: "The Lord prospers us on purpose, for a purpose." That is Truth!

But God...has a plan

CHAPTER SEVEN

BAPTISMS AND GIFTS OF THE SPIRIT

I want to share with you the highlights of our teaching, "The Three Baptisms for the Christian Today," which Rey and I taught at our Bible Study. First, we have the baptism into the Body of Christ, which is the "born again" experience. The only requirement for this baptism is that one is a repentant sinner. The agent that brings one into this experience is the Holy Spirit. The element into which the candidate is immersed is Jesus Christ. The purpose of this baptism is for the salvation of the soul and spirit. Born again by the Spirit of God, the candidate becomes a new creation in Christ Jesus.

The "born again" experience, I believe, is the biggest miracle any of us will ever realize. It is our gateway to all of what God has for us. It allows us to become His children, not just His creation. What a miracle that is! Now let's see what His Word says, shall we?

I also recommend you look these up and study them in the Amplified version of the Bible. It is lengthier, but gives you more detail on these Scriptures.

John 3: 1-21 NIV

Now there was a man of the Pharisees named Nicodemus, a member of the Jewish ruling council. 2 He came to Jesus at night and said, "Rabbi, we know you are a teacher who has come from God. For no one could perform the miraculous signs you are doing if God were not with him." 3 In reply Jesus declared, "I tell you the truth, no one can see the kingdom of God unless he is born again."4 "How can a man be born when he is old?" Nicodemus asked. "Surely he cannot enter a second time into his mother's womb to be born!" 5Jesus answered, "I tell you the truth, no one can enter the kingdom of God unless he is born of water and the Spirit.6 Flesh gives birth to flesh, but the Spirit gives birth to spirit. 7 You should not be surprised at my saying, 'You must be born again.' 8 The wind blows wherever it pleases. You hear its sound, but you cannot tell where it comes from or where it is going. So it is with everyone born of the Spirit." 9 "How can this be?" Nicodemus asked. 10 "You are Israel's teacher," said Jesus, "and do you not understand these things? 11 I tell you the truth, we speak of what we know, and we testify to what we have seen, but still you people do not accept our testimony. 12 I have spoken to you of earthly things and you do not believe; how then will you believe if I speak of heavenly things? 13No one has ever gone into heaven except the one who came from heaven — the Son of Man. 14 Just as Moses lifted up the snake in the desert, so the Son of Man must be lifted up, 15 that everyone who believes in him may have eternal life. 16 "For God so loved the world that he gave his one and only Son, that whoever believes in him shall not perish but have eternal life.
17 For God did not send his Son into the world to condemn the world, but to save the

world through him. ¹⁸ Whoever believes in him is not condemned, but whoever does not believe stands condemned already because he has not believed in the name of God's one and only Son. ¹⁹ This is the verdict: Light has come into the world, but men loved darkness instead of light because their deeds were evil. ²⁰Everyone who does evil hates the light, and will not come into the light for fear that his deeds will be exposed. ²¹ But whoever lives by the truth comes into the light, so that it may be seen plainly that what he has done has been done through God."

Rom. 6:3-7 NKJV
Or do you not know that as many of us as were baptized into Christ Jesus were baptized into His death? 4 Therefore we were buried with Him through baptism into death, that just as Christ was raised from the dead by the glory of the Father, even so we also should walk in newness 5 For if we have been united together in the likeness of His death, certainly we also shall be in the likeness of His resurrection, 6 knowing this, that our old man was crucified with Him, that the body of sin might be done away with, that we should no longer be slaves of sin. 7 For he who has died has been freed from sin.

1 Cor. 12:13 NKJV
For by one Spirit we were all baptized into one body — whether Jews or Greeks, whether slaves or free — and have all been made to drink into one Spirit.

2 Cor. 5:17 NKJV
Therefore, if anyone is in Christ, he is a new creation;
old things have passed away; behold, all things have
become new.

Gal. 3:27 NKJV
For as many of you as were baptized into Christ
have put on Christ.

Gal. 6:15-16 NKJV
For in Christ Jesus neither circumcision nor
uncircumcision avails anything,
but a new creation. 16 And as many as walk
according to this
rule, peace and mercy be upon them,
and upon the Israel of God.

Col. 2:12 NKJV
...buried with Him in baptism, in which you also
were raised with Him through faith in the working of God,
who raised Him from the dead.

The second baptism for the Christian today that I want to address is the Spirit baptism, referred to as the "Baptism into the Holy Spirit." This baptism is for the purpose of enabling the believer to receive two kinds of power: the Power of Authority and the Power of Ability, to do the work of God and to be God's witnesses.

The only requirement for this gift to be given us is that we be born again by the Spirit of God, which was the baptism we just covered. This is necessary to enable us to be filled with the precious gift of the baptism in the Holy Spirit. There is also no necessity for a lapse of

116

time, as it can come immediately, as soon as we ask for it after being born again. That is good news! The agent of this baptism is Jesus Christ. He is the Baptizer! Jesus Himself immerses us into the Holy Spirit for the purpose of being His witnesses.

Matt. 20:22-23 NKJV
But Jesus answered and said, "You do not know what you ask. Are you able to drink the cup that I am about to drink, and be baptized with the baptism that I am baptized with?" They said to Him, "We are able." 23 So He said to them, "You will indeed drink My cup, and be baptized with the baptism that I am baptized with;* but to sit on My right hand and on My left is not Mine to give, but it is for those for whom it is prepared by My Father."

Mark 1:8 NKJV
I indeed baptized you with water, but He will baptize you with the Holy Spirit." Mark 10:38-39 NKJV But Jesus said to them, "You do not know what you ask. Are you able to drink the cup that I drink, and be baptized with the baptism that I am baptized with?" 39 They said to Him, "We are able." So Jesus said to them "You will indeed drink the cup that I drink, and with the baptism I am baptized with you will be baptized;

Luke 3:16 NKJV
16 John answered, saying to all,"I indeed baptize you with water; but One mightier than I is coming, whose sandal strap I am not worthy to loose. He will baptize you with the Holy Spirit and fire.

Luke 7:37-39 NKJV
And behold, a woman in the city who was a sinner, when she knew that Jesus sat at the table in the Pharisee's House, brought an alabaster flask of fragrant oil, 38 and stood at His feet behind Him weeping; and she began to wash His feet with her tears, and wiped them with the hair of her head; and she kissed His feet and anointed them with the fragrant oil. 39 Now when the Pharisee who had invited Him saw this, he spoke to himself, saying, "This Man, if He were a prophet, would know who and what manner of woman this is who is touching Him, for she is a sinner."

Acts 1:5 NKJV
...for John truly baptized with water, but you shall be baptized with the Holy Spirit not many days from now."

Acts 2:4-6 NKJV
And they were all filled with the Holy Spirit and began to speak with other tongues, as the Spirit gave them utterance.5 And there were dwelling in Jerusalem Jews, devout men, from every nation under heaven. 6 And when this sound occurred, the multitude came together, and were confused, because everyone heard them speak in his own language.

Acts 2:38-39 NKJV
Then Peter said to them, "Repent, and let every one of you be baptized in the name of Jesus Christ for the remission of sins; and you shall receive the gift of the Holy Spirit. 39 For the promise is to you and to your children, and to all who are afar off, as many as the Lord our God will call."

Acts 10:45-46 NKJV
And those of the circumcision who believed were astonished, as many as came with Peter, because the gift of the Holy Spirit had been poured out on the Gentiles also. ⁴⁶ For they heard them speak with tongues and magnify God.

Acts 19:2-6 NKJV
He said to them, "Did you receive the Holy Spirit when you believed?" So they said to Him,"We have not so much as heard whether there is a Holy Spirit." ³ And he said to them, "Into what then were you baptized?" So they said, "Into John's baptism." ⁴ Then Paul said, "John indeed baptized with a baptism of repentance, saying to the people that they should believe on Him who would come after him, that is, on Christ Jesus." ⁵ When they heard this, they were baptized in the name of the Lord Jesus. ⁶ And when Paul had laid hands on them, the Holy Spirit came upon them, and they spoke with tongues and prophesied.

Those are such beautiful scriptures and so clearly delineate being born into Christ ("born again") and the baptism in the Holy Spirit as two separate and distinct occurrences.

Now there is one more baptism that I want to share and it is also very important: water baptism. This must be done after being born again but can be done before or after being immersed in the Holy Spirit. Many people are immersed in the Holy Spirit simultaneously with being born again. For those people, water baptism is performed afterward, while others are immersed in the Holy Spirit simultaneously with water baptism. Finally, for others, it is three complete and separate occasions.

We must not put God in a box as to how and when we are immersed into the Holy Spirit, but we also do not want to neglect water baptism, as Jesus set the example for us. This baptism is indicative of us dying to our old self-nature, and being resurrected with Him in newness! It is a testimony to our friends and relatives, and an act for the whole world to see that we have made a commitment to Jesus Christ and our intent to follow Him. It is a baptism showing our declaration of repentance and faith in Jesus Christ to our peers.

Matt. 28:19 NKJV
Go therefore and make disciples of all the nations,
baptizing them in the name of the Father and of the
Son and of the Holy Spirit,

Mark 16:16 NKJV
He who believes and is baptized will be saved; but he who does not
believe will be condemned.

Acts 2:38-41 NKJV
Then Peter said to them, "Repent, and let every one
of you be baptized in the name of Jesus Christ for the remission of
sins; and you shall receive the gift of the Holy Spirit. 39 For
the promise is to you and to your children, and to all who are afar
off, as many as the Lord our God will call." 40 And with many
other words he testified and exhorted them, saying, "Be saved
from this perverse generation." 41 Then those who gladly received his word were baptized; and that day about three thousand souls were added to them.

Acts 8:12-16 NKJV
But when they believed Philip as he preached the things concerning the kingdom of God and the name
of Jesus Christ, both men and women were baptized.

13 *Then Simon himself also believed; and when he was baptized*
he continued with Philip, and was amazed,
seeing the miracles and signs which were done. 14
Now when the apostles who were at Jerusalem heard that Samaria
had received the word of God, they sent
Peter and John to them, 15 *who, when they had come down,*
prayed for them that they might receive the Holy Spirit. 16 *For*
as yet He had fallen upon none of them. They had only been bap-
tized in the name of the Lord Jesus

Acts 8:36-40 NKJV
Now as they went down the road, they came to some water. And
the eunuch said, "See, here is water. What hinders me from being
baptized?" 37 *Then Philip said, "If you believe with all your*
heart, you may." And he answered and said, "I believe that Jesus
Christ is the Son of God." 38 *So he commanded the chariot to*
stand still. And both Philip and the eunuch went down into the
water, and he baptized him. 39 *Now when they came up out of*
the water, the Spirit of the Lord caught Philip away, so that the
eunuch saw him no more; and he went on his way rejoicing. 40
But Philip was found at Azotus. And passing through, he
preached in all the cities till he came to Caesarea.

Acts 9:18 NKJV
Immediately there fell from his eyes something like
scales, and he received his sight at once; and he arose and
was baptized.

Acts 10:47 NKJV
"Can anyone forbid water, that these should not be
baptized who have received the Holy Spirit just as we have?"

Acts 16:15 NKJV
And when she and her household were baptized, she begged
us, saying, "If you have judged me to be faithful
to the Lord, come to my house and stay." So she persuaded
us.

Acts 16:33 NKJV
And he took them the same hour of the night and washed
their stripes. And immediately he and all his family
were baptized.

Acts 18:8 NKJV
Then Crispus, the ruler of the synagogue, believed on the Lord
with his entire household. And many of the Corinthians, hearing,
believed and were baptized.

Acts 19:5 NKJV
When they heard this, they were baptized in the name of
the Lord Jesus.

1 Cor. 1:13-17 NKJV
"Is Christ divided? Was Paul crucified for you? Or were you bap-
tized in the name of Paul? 14 I thank God that I baptized none of
you except Crispus and Gaius, 15 lest anyone should say that
I had baptized in my own name. 16 Yes, I also baptized
the household of Stephanas. Besides, I do not know whether
I baptized any other. 17 For Christ did not send me to baptize,
but to preach the gospel, not with wisdom of words, lest the cross
of Christ should be made of no effect.

These scriptures show the different ways that people were baptized in water. As I mentioned before, some were baptized before Holy Spirit baptism, some received the two simultaneously and others are after water baptism. So, all three are scriptural. Paul was leaving the baptizing in water up to the local church after he had evangelized. Therefore, he was addressing the fact that he was not personally baptizing his converts. Not all churches practice immersion today, but I do not find in the scripture that it was practiced any other way. I will not quarrel about that point, but it is how I personally understand the scriptures.

I have been born again, baptized in the Holy Spirit and then water baptized. Our church did not have a baptismal facility, so we had to go to a local body of water. It was not practical to baptize each person at the exact time of his or her born again experience. That is true of most churches today that practice immersion. My experience happened when I was nine and a half years old, but I will never forget it; it was a very memorable experience. Later in my adult life, I had the privilege of being baptized in the River Jordan in Israel. That, too, was a memorable experience. It was certainly not necessary to be baptized a second time; it was just a personal choice.

We should pray in the Holy Spirit every day. It is like being baptized in the Holy Spirit on a continual basis. It keeps us in tune with the Spirit and enables us to hear from Him more clearly. It also means we are always praying a perfect prayer, as it is the Holy Spirit praying through us, a willing vessel, to get God's will done in our lives and for others we have been assigned to intercede for!

Along with the baptism in the Holy Spirit come certain gifts that the Holy Spirit wishes to give as He deems appropriate. How many times have you heard: "You should have been there? I saw the gifts of God manifested!" But which gifts were they? And what difference does it make which gift was manifested?

To the one who has received the gift, it does not make a bit of difference - that person received! But to you, the one who is operating in the gifts of the Holy Spirit, with Holy Spirit boldness and with Holy Spirit power, you must know the difference in power, between the natural actions of man and the supernatural manifestations of God. *Zech 4:6b, Not by might, nor by power, but by my spirit, saith the LORD of hosts.* An excellent example of this life-changing power of God is the awesome sudden change of Peter found in the Book of Acts.

My main objective for this teaching is to help equip you to be fully able to operate in all of the gifts of the Holy Spirit. Our purpose here on the earth is to fulfill the Great Commission and to do all the works of the Father. As He is, so are we in this world.

1 John 4:17 NKJV

Love has been perfected among us in this: that we may have boldness in the Day of Judgment; because as He is, so are we in this world.

Mark 16:15-20 NKJV

And He said to them, Go into all the world and preach the gospel to every creature. 16 He who believes and is baptized will be saved; but he who does not believe will be condemned. 17 And these signs will follow those who believe: In My name they will cast out demons; they will speak with new tongues; 18 they will take up serpents; and if they drink anything deadly, it will by no means hurt them; they will lay hands on the sick, and they will recover." 19 So then, after the Lord *had spoken to them, He was received up into heaven, and sat down at the right hand of God. 20 And they went out and preached everywhere, the Lord working with them and confirming the word through the accompanying signs. Amen.*

Isa. 61:1-2 NKJV
"The Spirit of the Lord GOD IS upon Me, Because the
LORD has anointed Me To preach good tidings to the poor;
He has sent Me to heal the brokenhearted, To proclaim liber-
ty to the captives, And the opening of the prison to those who are
bound; 2 To proclaim the acceptable year of the LORD , And
the day of vengeance of our God; To comfort all who mourn,

Luke 4:18-19 NKJV
"The Spirit of the LORD is upon Me, Because He has
anointed Me To preach the gospel to the poor; He has sent Me to
heal the brokenhearted, To proclaim liberty to the captives And
recovery of sight to the blind, To set at liberty those who are op-
pressed; 19 To proclaim the acceptable year of the LORD "

We can operate in all of the Gifts of The Holy
Spirit, just as Paul did. God (Jesus) will give them to anyone
who seeks, hungers and thirsts for more of God, because
God is no respecter of persons. He does not play favorites.
He will give you what you need. The more you hunger and
thirst, the more He will pour out on you!

Acts 10:34 NKJV
Then Peter opened his mouth and said: "In truth I
perceive that God shows no partiality".

We must fully understand and believe that the
manifestations of the Gifts of The Holy Spirit are for the
common good! *(1 Cor. 12:7 Now to each one the manifestation*
of the Spirit is given for the common good. NIV)

The Nine Gifts of the Holy Spirit
(Nine Manifestations)

Please take notice of what the "given article" is called in 1 Cor. 12:7. The "given article" is a "manifestation" -- a revelation of the Holy Spirit at that given moment and time for the purpose which He (the Holy Spirit) chooses to manifest.

1 Cor. 12:8-11 NKJV
...For to one is given the word of wisdom through the
Spirit, to another the word of knowledge through the same
Spirit, 9 to another faith by the same Spirit, to another gifts of
healings by the same Spirit, 10 to another the working of mir-
acles, to another prophecy, to another discerning of spirits, to
another different kinds of tongues, to another the interpreta-
tion of tongues. 11 But one and the same Spirit works all
these things, distributing to each one individually s
He wills.

I have actually heard it taught that we can only have one of the gifts, but if you read this carefully, you will see that it is talking about the individual person, not the individual gift. You can operate in all the gifts just as Apostle Paul did! He would not tell us to earnestly desire something that was not available to us!

1 Cor. 12:31a NKJV
But earnestly desire the best gifts. And yet I show you a more ex-
cellent way.

The Manifestation Of The Holy Spirit Has Three Categories:

Gifts of Power
These are the three gifts the Holy Spirit chooses to operate through the believer <u>to do something.</u>

1. Gift of Faith (Great Faith - God's Faith)
2. Gift of Working Miracles (Miraculous Powers)
3. Gift of Healings (Notice this is plural)

Gifts of Utterance
These are the three gifts the Holy Spirit uses through the believer <u>to tell something</u>.

1. Gift of Prophecy (Foretelling & "Forth Telling")
2. Gift of Speaking In Tongues (Speaking to God)
3. Gift of Interpretation of Tongues (Edification)

Gifts of Revelation
These are the three gifts that the Holy Spirit uses through the believer <u>to reveal something.</u>

1. Gift of The Word of Wisdom (Present/Future)
2. Gift of The Word of Knowledge (Past)
3. Gift of The Discerning of Spirits (Good or Evil)

It is important to understand that the "Gift of the Holy Spirit" in Acts 2:4; 8; 2:38; 8:12-17; 10:45; 19:2-16 is **not** one of the nine gifts of the Holy Spirit. Jesus gives us the Gift of The Holy Spirit and the Holy Spirit enables us with His nine gifts! Isn't that exciting to know?

God IS Love and, without Love, none of the gifts can work as they are meant to work! Go back and reread the chapter on love. LOVE is the POWER that makes the "GIFTS" function. (Love is power, not fear!)

2 Tim. 1:7 KJV

For God hath not given us the spirit of fear; but of power, and of love, and of a sound mind.

1 Cor. 1:7-9 NKJV

...so that you come short in no gift, eagerly waiting for the revelation of our Lord Jesus Christ, 8 who will also confirm you to the end, that you may be blameless in the day of our Lord Jesus Christ. 9 God is faithful, by whom you were called into the fellowship of His Son, Jesus Christ our Lord.

1 Cor. 2:9-14 (NIV)

However, as it is written: "No eye has seen, no ear has heard, no mind has conceived what God has prepared for those who love him"-- 10 but God has revealed it to us by his Spirit. The Spirit searches all things, even the deep things of God. 11 For who among men knows the thoughts of a man except the man's spirit within him? In the same way no one knows the thoughts of God except the Spirit of God.

12 We have not received the spirit of the world but The Spirit who is from God, that we may understandwhat God has freely given us. 13 This is what we speak, not in words taught us by human wisdom but in words taught by the Spirit, expressing spiritual truths in spiritual words. 14 The man without the Spirit does not accept the things that come from the Spirit of God, for they are foolishness to him, and he cannot understand them, because they are spiritually discerned.

It has come to me through the prophetic word that 1Corinthians 12: 9-10 outlines the gifts that God has given to me. I received that word and have operated in some of those gifts on many occasions. I expect to do so more and more, as the Word says to earnestly desire the gifts, and I sure do desire them! The gifts in verse 8 also work in conjunction with the gifts in 9 and 10. The Holy Spirit gives these gifts to us. They are His gifts to be given out at His pleasure and His will. That is why it is so important to be baptized into Holy Spirit, as that is the door opener to the gifts. At the same time, we must be walking in love to have these gifts working at their maximum!

The Gift of Healings was first activated in me when I was between nine and ten years old. I was filled with the Spirit at nine and a half and it was soon after that when I started operating in the gift of healings. No one laid hands on me to receive this gift, but God deposited it into me by His sovereign will.

I mentioned this before, but I want to address it again, as I consider it very important. Mother Potter had extreme headaches. What they called "sick headaches" in those days, we usually refer to as migraines today. The moment I would lay hands on her, they would disappear. I have heard people speak disparagingly about "just faith enough for headaches," but I want to tell you as one who has suffered from migraines, it is no little thing to the one who is suffering! It was one of the greatest miracles in my life when God healed me of that onerous malady!

The Gift of Healings continued to grow in my life. I do not know that I remember all of the times it was manifested, but I cannot ever forget the time that Bill's lung was healed. It was supposed to be removed because of an irreparable hole that it had in it. They had given him only a ten percent chance of surviving the surgery, as it was his second surgery on the same lung. God had other plans! I shared that in another portion of this book. Some miracles need to be repeated!

I have always considered healings to be my primary gift, but I am not certain that is necessarily so at this stage of my life! It is amazing what we can see in retrospect! When we experience creative healings, those are miracles!

The Gift of Discerning of Spirits is a must-have for Christians today! We need to know what we are dealing with in the human spirit, as well as in the second heaven. Of course, this gift is not limited to evil spirits, but contention originates in evil spirits. We need to understand and be able to separate the spirit from the individual. We are not contending with people, but with the spirit that dominates them.

The Lord is so gracious with His gifts. He enables us to discern the good in people. By discerning the Spirit of Good, we can often ascertain their gifts. But the Discerning of Spirits also enables us to determine any evil spirit for which the individual needs deliverance. He protects us time after time! The Gift of Discerning of Spirits is very important for the believer!

Eph. 6:12 AMP
*For we are not wrestling with flesh and blood [contending on-
ly with physical opponents], but against the despotisms,
against the powers, against [the master spirits who are] the
world rulers of this present darkness, against the spirit forces of wickedness in the heavenly (supernatural) sphere.*

I am not exactly sure what category some of the gifts
I have been given would fall into, but they are gifts of God
nonetheless. I suppose they would fall into words of
knowledge and words of wisdom. We cannot put God in a
box with any of His gifts, but just flow with Him as He di-
rects; whichever one He is choosing to use at any given
moment!

When God uploaded into me a complete
knowledge of accounting, including cost accounting, and
the management skills that I needed, it was knowledge
equivalent to a college degree. I operated in that very high
level for over fifty years! I was able to train others in
the knowledge that I was given as well.Revelation
knowledge can be given to us for both practical and spiritual reasons.

Many times in business meetings, I opened my
mouth to speak and the words that flowed out were
not my words, but came straight from the Holy Spirit.
Others were unaware of this, of course, but I knew! They
carried great insight and wisdom and were apropos for the
subject at hand. The Holy Spirit also directed me where
to find lost files and helped me a great deal with time management. He truly is our helper! He is not limited in
any way whatsoever! We only need to humbly ask
Him for His help! You see, I learned a long time ago, that

if a thing is important to me, it is important to Him. I am not ashamed to ask for even the smallest of things!

Back in the eighties, when I wore contact lens, I had just gotten a new pair. Each lens replacement was seventy-five dollars. I lost one of mine at home shortly after I had gotten them. I had exhausted my efforts in looking for it, and Rey's efforts as well! I had prayed for healing of my eyes, but had no manifestation. I flopped down in my chair, very disgusted, and said, "Lord, if you are not going to heal my eyes at this time, the least you can do is help me find my lost contact lens, so that I don't have to pay another seventy-five dollars!" You would think God would ignore that kind of approach but no, He replied, "Go in the kitchen and look under the (movable) bar."

I immediately responded. I found a piece of hard plastic that appeared to be the kind certain capsules came in. It looked nothing like a little contact lens. The Lord instructed me to place it in my contact lens solution case and leave it, so I did! He then had me go back a couple hours later to put them in my eyes. When I opened my case, there was the lens with the perfect fit and prescription.

Now, I do not know to this day if it was in fact the lens, or if God made it into the lens, but it really did not matter. Either way, it had been a personal miracle from My Father! I have had many similar experiences in my lifetime, and they never cease to amaze me. He shows me His love in so many ways.

Another gift that is very profound is the Gift of Faith. This is not the ordinary measure of faith that you use on a daily basis, but it is the faith that our Father drops into us on certain occasions that we know, that we know, that we know a thing! It is His Faith in us.

An example of this is one I related to you already but I want to point it out again: the incident of my tumbling down the stairs when I was at my daughter, Zoe Leeta's, home. That was the Gift of Faith in action. They wanted to immediately take me to urgent care. I declined, as the Gift of Faith had risen up in me, and I knew that I knew I was all right. Without that gift of faith that dropped into me, I would have gladly gone to the doctor to be checked out, but I KNEW I was okay! It also enabled me to walk the distance I needed to walk.

When The Gift of Faith is present, you do not need to be told, you just know it! It is God's Faith that He gives us for a particular purpose at a certain time. Many times the Gift of Faith works in conjunction with our other gifts. In my case, it is the Gift of Healings that it works alongside of, for my ministry. What a Blessing!

THESE THINGS ARE VITAL FOR US TO KNOW:

❖ TO BELIEVE THAT THE POWER IS IN THE WORD OF GOD. (Read Mark 4:1-34)

❖ IF GOD SAID IT, IT WILL SURELY COME TO PASS.

Isa. 55:11
So shall my word be that goeth forth out of my mouth: it shall not return unto me void, but it shall accomplish that which I please, and it shall prosper in the thing whereto I sent it.

❖ TO HAVE EXPECTATION OF
THE MANIFESTATION OF HOLY SPIRIT.

Acts 3:5
And he gave heed unto them, expecting to receive
Something of them

❖ WE MUST SPEAK THE WORD BOLDLY
AND WITH POWER.

Acts 2:14 KJV
But Peter, standing up with the eleven, lifted up his voice,
and said unto them, "Ye men of Judaea, and all ye that dwell at
Jerusalem, be this known unto you, and hearken
to my words:

Acts 4:29-31 (NIV)
29 Now, Lord, consider their threats and enable
your servants to speak your word with great bold-
ness. 30 Stretch out your hand to heal and perform
miraculous signs and wonders through the name of your
holy servant Jesus." 31 After they prayed, the place where
they were meeting was shaken.
And they were all filled with the Holy Spirit and
spoke the word of God boldly.

Jn. 14:12 NIV
I tell you the truth; anyone who has faith in me will do what I
have been doing. He will do even greater things than these, be-
cause I am going to the Father.

❖ GOD IS NO RESPECTER OF PERSONS

Acts 10:34 AMP
And Peter opened his mouth and said: Most
certainly and thoroughly I now perceive and understand that God
shows no partiality and is no respecter of persons,

❖ WE MUST BE FULLY PERSUADED THAT GOD
HAS POWER TO DO WHAT HE HAS PROMISED.
God said it-that's it!

Rom. 4:21 NIV
being fully persuaded that God had power to do what
he had promised.

❖ WE MUST STIR UP THE GIFTS THAT ARE
WITHIN US.

2 Tim. 1:6 KJV
Wherefore I put thee in remembrance that thou stir up
the gift of God, which is in thee by the putting on of my hands.

1 Cor. 1:4-7 KJV
I thank my God always on your behalf, for the grace of od which is
given you by Jesus Christ; 5 That in everything ye are enriched
by him, in all utterance, and in all knowledge; 6 Even as the tes-
timony of Christ was confirmed in you 7 So that ye come behind
in no gift; waiting for the coming of our Lord Jesus Christ.

Mark 4:11 NIV
11 He told them, "The secret of the kingdom of God has been
given to you. But to those on the outside everything is said
in parables

Eph. 1:9 KJV
9 Having made known unto us the mystery of his will, according
to his good pleasure which he hath purposed
in himself:

Another important point in conjunction with spiritual gifts is with regard to the Armor of God. Most people are familiar with the six pieces of God's armor as listed in Eph. 6:15-17, but neglect to read about the seventh piece of armor. It is the best way to pray for our fellow believers (saints): praying in the spirit. This is the seventh piece of God's armor.

We owe it to each other to intercede. Intercession is a powerful tool for the believer! Lives and circumstances are changed through Intercession.

Eph 6:18 KJV
...praying always with all prayer and supplication in the
Spirit, being watchful to this end with all perseverance
and supplication for all the saints —

Rom. 8:26-27 NKJV
26 Likewise the Spirit also helps in our weaknesses. For we do not
know what we should pray for as we ought, but the Spirit Himself
makes intercession for us with groanings which cannot be uttered.
27 Now He who searches the hearts knows what the mind of the

Spirit is, because He makes intercession for the saints according to the will of God.

We cannot read this scripture and not understand the power of intercession!

But God...has a plan

RABBIT TRAILS

CHAPTER EIGHT

FRUIT OF THE SPIRIT

Gal. 5:22-23 NKJV
But the fruit of the Spirit is love, joy, peace, *longsuffering, kindness, goodness, faithfulness,* 23 *gentleness, self-control. Against such there is no law.*

Gal 5:22-23 AMP
But the fruit of the [Holy] Spirit [the work which His presence within accomplishes] is love, joy (gladness), peace, patience (an even temper, forbearance), kindness, goodness (benevolence), faithfulness, 23 *Gentleness (meekness, humility), self-control (self-restraint, continence).*
*Against such things there is no law [*z*that can bring a charge].*

While it is important that we operate in the gifts of the Holy Spirit, if we do not have the fruit of the Holy Spirit abounding in our lives, the effect of the gifts is greatly diminished. I cannot stress this enough! We need to practice the fruit of the spirit until it becomes not our "second nature," but our "first nature."

It will just automatically be the first thing we do, which I know is against the sin nature. But remember we are no longer slaves to our sin nature!

Rom. 6:6   NIV
For we know that our old self was crucified with him so that the body of sin might be done away with, that we should no longer be slaves to sin —

Gal. 5:6 NKJV
For in Christ Jesus neither circumcision nor uncircumcision avails anything, but faith working through love.

Rom. 6:18 AMP
And having been set free from sin, you have become the servants of righteousness (of conformity to the divine will in thought, purpose, and action)

So, since our faith is to be working through love and we have been set free from sin, walking in the fruit of the spirit should be our first nature! This does not come overnight, however. We must intentionally practice! Practice on purpose!

A few years ago, as I was studying Galatians 5:22, The Lord spoke to me and said, "Do you see how each fruit builds on each other? I designed it that way."

I saw immediately what He was showing me.   It became revelation to me and I was so excited. Yes, when we have developed love, we have joy! When we have love and joy, we then have peace. Then comes patience, or longsuffering, which enables us to have kindness and goodness, then faithfulness and gentleness! And, lastly and very importantly, we will have self-control!

You may wonder why self-control is at the end of the list, when it is so important, and can get us into so much trouble if we do not exercise it. If we have developed all of that other fruit in our lives, we will have enabled ourselves to have self-control!

When God revealed this to me, I thought, "Wow, this is so good that He would show this to me!" About three to four weeks later, a brother in the Lord taught about the exact same thing on television, and I knew there was the probability that I had gotten the revelation at the same time this brother was taping his broadcast! No time and distance in God, is there? He was telling me the same thing He was telling others, and it was a great confirmation of the revelation He had given to me! To me, it was all for me! There could have been thousands more out there experiencing the same thing, but so what? I only knew that what I had heard from God had been confirmed to me!

Without love, we cannot experience joy! Without love and joy, we cannot experience peace in our lives! When we do not have peace, we cannot have patience or longsuffering (forbearance with others). If we are devoid of patience or longsuffering with others, we will be unkind and not good to others. We will be unable to be faithful to a cause and gentleness will be non-existent in our lives.

When we meet people that are cranky and mean-spirited, we can know full well they are unhappy and not at peace. Patience is my dominant characteristic strength, and, believe me, it has served me well. I have many occasions to practice and work on this Fruit of the Spirit.

Working with others requires a great deal of this fruit! I see the Fruit on a tree and as we pick the Fruit from that tree, more must be grown to replace it, so that we have a never-ending supply! We have a "fruitful" orchard!

Self-control? Automatic? I think not! If we are not growing and manifesting the other Fruit, I believe our whole life will be out of control! BUT if we have an abundance of all the other Fruit, we will be self- controlled! After all, our self-control is really by the power of Holy Spirit control!

Gal. 5:25 AMP
If we live by the [Holy] Spirit, let us also walk by the Spirit. [If by the Holy Spirit we have our life in God, let us go forward walking in line, our conduct controlled by the Spirit.]

Gal. 5:25 NIV
Since we live by the Spirit, let us keep in step with the Spirit.

I believe this to be a command from God rather than a suggestion. He has given us everything we need to carry out His instructions. He asks us to do nothing that He has not enabled us to do.

Having the Fruit of the Spirit in our lives will enable us to walk in the Spirit. I really like the way it reads in the NIV version because, to me, it is saying: "lock-step." Now that is just a personal revelation to me of that scripture, but I see myself marching along in lock step with the Holy Spirit and I find that very exciting! If we walk in lock step, we will not stray from His path! We will not get off on as many wrong Rabbit Trails of life!

We are soldiers, in the army of God. We are one

army, made up of many segments. I don't like to use the word divisions, since we are not to be a divided army, as we have a single purpose. Our purpose is to do His will, whatever He reveals to us to do ! We have different callings with different platforms, but it takes the same fruit in our lives to accomplish this purpose.

We must have these elements at work to be suc- cessful in our call: love, joy, peace, patience (longsuffer- ing), kindness, goodness, faithfulness, gentleness and self- control. I just love looking at this line- up; it is so challeng- ing! Can you imagine the difference if every child of God were walking in this as we are instructed, every moment of every day, in every way? I know, we think this is impossible! But would our Father request of us some- thing impossible to do, when He has already said, "With God, all things are possible?" We know He would not. Our own insecurities keep us from experiencing the blessings of walking in this place of security with Him, that only He can provide.

Some years ago, Rey and I had gone to Sacramento on business and, when we arrived at the airport, our fel- low businessman, with whom we were meeting, picked us up at the airport. As we were walking to the vehicle, I re- alized he must have parked a long way off! Then we walked into the private plane area and I realized he was taking us to his plane. I had never, nor did I ever want to, ride in a private plane. I also realized I could not say this aloud, as it would be a bad confession of my faith since we had been witnessing to this man. I said a silent prayer of "Lord, help me!"

The Lord's response to that prayer was awe- some. He merely said to me: "I am the same God in the air as I am on the ground." I boarded the plane knowing I would be safe! My Papa was in control, not me! I call God "Father" most of the time, I guess, but I do have many "Papa" moments. Sometimes I have "Daddy" moments, as well! Sometimes I just crawl up onto Daddy's lap and talk to Him. Don't you love the privileges afforded to us as His children? This was definitely a "Daddy" moment.

Gal. 4:6 NIV
Because you are sons, God sent the Spirit of his Son into our hearts, the Spirit who calls out, "Abba, Father."

I challenge you to make a concerted effort to grow this Fruit in your life and let it fully develop, so that you can enjoy all the benefits and have your own life in control. I know people who are always trying to get someone else's life in control when they need to be working on their own life! Let's work on our own life until we get it right!

When we reach the point where all is in control, we come to realize that it is He who is really in control! So let us walk in the fear and admonition of the Lord. When we do that, He has the issues of our lives under control.

I like what I learned from Pastor Kenny Gatlin. He says, "The fear of the Lord is to hate what God hates and to love what God loves." Simple enough that we can all understand it, isn't it ?

CHAPTER NINE

HEARING GOD:
HEAR, DO AND SEE

Phil 4:8-9 KJV
Finally, brethren, whatsoever things are true, whatsoever things are honest, whatsoever things are just, whatsoever things are pure, whatsoever things are lovely, whatsoever things are of good report; if there be any virtue, and if there be any praise, think on these things.9 Those things, which ye have both learned, and received, and heard, and seen in me, do: and the God of peace shall be with you

After all I have written, I question what more to write concerning hearing from God. I don't want to relate the same experiences over again, yet so much of my life and experiences are grounded in my hearing from God. Many times I have spoken things and actually surprised myself by what I said. I know those were God's words, not my words. I have never heard the audible voice of God speak to me, other than my name being called on occasion, and of course the open vision I had as a child. He speaks to me in my heart on a regular basis. Usually He speaks very softly, but if I do not respond to the soft promptings, He can get more forceful in His promptings to me!

I love it when He speaks through me, in the business environment and I am as surprised as anyone by what comes out. Of course, He and I are the only ones who know this on most occasions. This has happened to me frequently in Business meetings and Department Head meetings, etc.

The Lord can make us look so brilliant at times; it neverceases to amaze me! This works well for a business person, but of course He was the one who set me on that path, so it only made sense that He continue to bless me in it for all those years. It appears that the season of the automobile business has now ended for me, but I do not know this as a fact.

He not only speaks to us about spiritual things, but about practical things as well. We just need to be open and listen and allow Him full access. He will use us at any time, in any place, as long as we have an open heart and a willingness to listen and obey Him. We need to keep our receiver tuned to God's frequency.

Once we hear from God, it is important that we understand (or see) what it is He is saying to us. In my personal experience, it has been necessary many times that I just allow God to arise in me and give me backbone to say (or do) what would not be normal for me. It is good that I am not in the confrontational mode all the time, but there are occasions when God needs me to rise up and be heard! It is against my human nature, so I am very aware of it!

So it was when I left the first job God gave me when He uploaded my education into me. I am very quiet and soft spoken by nature. I am a very non- confrontational person. (Although I must admit I have had a quietly rebellious streak at times.) As I shared with you in a previous chapter, when my new owner was asking me to do something that I knew was wrong, I refused to do it. My reaction was totally out of character for me when I stood up and threw the large stack of documents at him, telling him that if he wanted them put on the books he could do it himself! I shocked myself. Righteous indignation is a mighty force!

I have a few people who call me for support and when that happens the Holy Spirit gives me the insight to share with them and they usually receive the confirmation they need. Afterward, I ponder what I have shared and realize many times it is advice that I need to implement for myself! I feel certain I am not the only person that ministers one-on-one that experiences personal ministry from the Holy Spirit in the process! That really helps us to hear from the Holy Spirit. Then there are times when the Holy Spirit speaks to us with just a scripture reference, as I shared with you on the Jeremiah 29:11 revelation. That scripture will forever be personal to me!

Jer. 29:11 NIV
For I know the plans I have for you," declares the LORD, "plans to prosper you and not to harm you, plans to give you hope and a future.

However, the way He showed me 2 Cor. 1:20 was entirely different. The Lord trained me for business so

He often shows me things from that perspective. As I was studying one day, preparing a teaching for a women's meeting, 2 Cor 1:20 was a part of my text.

2 Cor. 1:20 NIV
For no matter how many promises God has made, they are Yes" in Christ. And so through him the "Amen" is spoken by us to the glory of God.

Suddenly in the Spirit I saw a business bank check that required two signatures. It was a blank check payable to "you" drawn on the Bank Of Heaven, but God, the Father, had already signed it. The Spirit spoke to me and explained that when we said the "Amen," or yes, we were counter-signing with the Father and the check was negotiable. It could be made out for whatever the need was: healing, deliverance, finances, or any other need.

Recently, I was recounting that revelation to my friend, and suddenly I had increased revelation of that vision! He spoke to me and said, "Remember that on some occasions the bank would cash a check with only one signature that carried more authority than two others together?" I acknowledged what He was saying, and He went on, "Sometimes in my sovereignty I will provide for someone before they even are aware of me, because it brings awareness and serves a higher purpose. Also, on some occasions, two persons with lesser authority can sign together and it carries the same authority and is also cashable. This is for 'When any two agree!'" I got it! I got it! His promises are always "YES!" He has multiple ways of negotiating answers for us. We ain't seen nothin' yet!

But God...has a plan

Matt. 18:19 KJV
"Again, I tell you that if two of you on earth agree
about anything you ask for, it will be done for you by my
Father in heaven."

Listening to the Holy Spirit and responding to Him is so very vital. In the case of my friend's son, "B," whom I needed to intercede for on that Sunday night at 11:20 p.m., it was a matter of life or death.

In other situations, it may save us time and frustration. It has happened so many times in the work place, but I will give one example of what might seem like a trifling matter. We needed a letter, which someone had brought into my office earlier, and laid it on my desk. I couldn't find it anywhere on my desk. I remembered that others had brought car deal folders (jackets) and laid them on my desk as well. One of my employees had picked them up later and filed them away. I felt certain this single piece of paper had been filed with one of these deals. They could not remember the names on these files. We had approximately ten five-drawer cabinets in our file room for car deals alone. There were far too many to go through.

I went into the ladies' room and talked to the Lord. He very simply spoke a name to me. I went back into the office and straight to the file cabinets, looked up that name, and there in that folder was the paper that I needed! It had indeed been filed in one of those folders by mistake. Without the help of the Holy Spirit, I would never have found that letter that I so desperately needed.

There have been many instances where He has come to my rescue and has helped me over and over and over again. He has no limit on His "Help Line"! I can never praise Him enough! The Holy Spirit is not only a Spiritual Helper, but a practical Helper, as well.

Another incident happened some year's earlier when I was employed as a comptroller for a group of dealerships near my home. I had agreed to take over the Finance Department as manager on a temporary basis. It needed to be brought into compliance in several areas, so it could function better. I found we had sold a pickup and camper to a young couple who really did not qualify and no bank would finance them. I had many of these kinds of "deals" to try to clear up in the department!

Since we were unable to get them financed, the couple finally brought the vehicle back. By this time, the young man was uncooperative and refused to sign the necessary papers to cancel the sale. This procedure in the industry is called an "unwind." The young woman, who was not yet married to this young man, wanted to cooperate. My only other option would have been to handle it as repossession. She understood the dynamics of the consequences to their credit if they persisted in refusing to sign documents necessary for an unwind.

She came into my office, and I perceived in the Spirit that she was hurting. I chatted with her a bit; she signed the documents for me, and then just sat there! She was visibly unhappy with her life, and it had nothing to do with the vehicle transaction! I then asked her if I could talk to her as a friend and not as an employee of the dealership. She was more than ready to talk. I gently spoke with her, and after just a few minutes, I had led her to Jesus. I wanted to lead her into the baptism of The Holy Spirit, but I had other customers waiting to see me.

I invited her to my home Bible Study, which "happened" to be that night and she agreed to come.

At the Bible Study, she was baptized in The Holy Spirit and continued to attend each week. After growing in the Lord very quickly, she made the decision to return to her father's home in Michigan with her four-year-old son. She had severed her relationship with the young man by this time, and was serving The Lord whole-heartedly. When I last heard from her, she was going to church in Michigan and moving on with God! We have lost touch, but I still pray for her to stay on the path or-dained for her.

We must listen to God in every situation and take every opening He gives us to do His work! We must also wait for an answer when we ask His direction and not go ahead on certain actions without a clear word. At times, He will allow us to do things, but then we find out that it wasn't the best thing to do! We can learn through the process.

I am recalling the year 2005-2006 when I hired a landscaper. I was well into my house remodel at this time. The landscape architect had been referred to me and he professed to be a Christian. I did not wait on God for confirmation, and had many other things going on at the same time. Bottom line, that incident cost me over one hundred fifty thousand dollars and a long delay in putting my home on the market for sale.

In the meantime, real estate dropped in value, and my Palos Verdes home value decreased dramatically. That cost me several hundred thousand dollars as well. God, with the help of a friend, sold my property for me when others were not selling, but it was not for the amount I could have sold it for earlier. I would have been able to sow more into the Kingdom, if I had waited on

God. As it was, there was little equity. Of course, the landscape architect was long gone, but it re-affirmed to me that we must wait on God for an answer! I realize that my Father knew all about this long beforehand and allowed me to proceed on this path. He had visited all of my tomorrows and knew what lay ahead. He didn't scold me nor upbraid me and just continues His faithfulness to me.

The most profound experience I have had of hearing, doing and seeing is what I shared with you about Rey's conversion. That was an awesome experience with great rewards! We learn from our experiences, both favorable and unfavorable. It is what we do with the lessons He taught us, and how we respond, that really counts in the end!

But God...has a plan

CHAPTER TEN

CALLING AND SETTING APART

Matt. 22:14 NKJV
"For many are called, but few are chosen."

Matt. 22:14 AMP
For many are called (invited and summoned), but few are chosen.

God calls everyone unto Himself, but the chosen ones are those who have answered His call. The ones who have accepted His invitation to Salvation become the "chosen ones." Everyone should want to be a chosen one. But, sorrowfully, not all accept His call to repentance. When we accept His call, we are chosen to be His child, no longer just His creation.

Eph. 2:10 NIV
For we are God's workmanship, created in Christ Jesus to do good works, which God prepared in advance for us to do

Eph. 2:10 AMP
For we are God's [own] handiwork (His workmanship),recreated
in Christ Jesus, [born anew]
that we may do those good works which God predestined
(planned beforehand) for us [taking paths which He prepared
ahead of time], that we should walk in them [living the good life
which He prearranged and made ready for us to live].

When Hannah promised the Lord that she would give her child to Him, she meant business with God. From that moment Samuel was called of God! When he was old enough, she delivered him to the priest to be trained. So some time passed before Samuel was actually set apart as a priest unto God.

1 Sam. 2:35 NKJV
Then I will raise up for Myself a faithful priest who shall do according to what is in My heart and in My mind. I will build him a sure house, and he shall walk before My anointed forever.

So it can be with us today. We can have a calling on our life, separate from our calling to salvation, to do a specific work for the Lord. God establishes our gifts and callings before we are even born. He also establishes the generation we are to be born into, and then it could be weeks, months or even years before God sets us apart for the work He has pre-ordained for us to do.

Look at the scripture on Samuel. God was faithful and honored His word through Samuel. Since God knows us before the foundation of the world, He knows both our calling and the exact time that He has ordained. We are never a mistake!

154

1 Sam. 3:1-19 NKJV
Now the boy Samuel ministered to the LORD before Eli. no wide-
spread revelation. 2 And it came to pass at that time, while Eli
was lying down in his place, and when his eyes had begun to grow
so dim that he could not see,

3 and before the lamp of God went out in the tabernacle of the
LORD WHERE the ark of God was, and while Samuel was ly-
ing down, 4 that the LORD called Samuel. And he an-
swered, "Here I am!" 5 So he ran to Eli and said, "Here I am, for
you called me." And he said, "I did not call; lie down again."
And he went and lay down. 6 Then the LORD CALLED yet
again, "Samuel!" So Samuel arose and went to Eli, and said,
"Here I am, for you called me." He answered, "I did not
call, my son; lie down again." 7 (Now Samuel did not yet know
the LORD, nor was the word of the LORD YET revealed to him.)
8 And the LORD called Samuel again the third time. So he arose
and went to Eli, and said, "Here I am, for you did call me." Then
Eli perceived that the LORD

HAD called the boy. 9 Therefore Eli said to Samuel, "Go, lie
down; and it shall be, if He calls you, that you must say, 'Speak,
LORD, for Your servant hears.'" So Samuel went and lay
down in his place.10 Now the LORD CAME and stood and
called as at other times, "Samuel! Samuel!" And Samuel an-
swered, "Speak, for Your servant hears." 11 Then the LORD
SAID to

Samuel: "Behold, I will do something in Israel at which
both ears of everyone who hears it will tingle. 12 In that day
I will perform against Eli all that I have
spoken concerning his house, from beginning to end.
13 For I have told him that I will judge his house forever for
the iniquity which he knows, because his
sons made themselves vile, and he did not restrain them. 14
And therefore I have sworn to the house of Eli that the iniquity of

*Eli's house shall not be atoned for by s sacrifice or offering forever." 15 So Samuel lay down until morning, and opened the doors of the house of the LORD . And Samuel was afraid to tell Eli the vision.
16 Then Eli called Samuel and said, "Samuel, my son!" He answered, "Here I am." 17 And he said,
"What is the word that the LORD spoke to you? Please do not hide it from me. God do so to you, and more also, if you hide anything from me of all the things that He said to you." 18 Then Samuel told him everything, and hid nothing from him. And he said, "It is the LORD. Let Him do what seems good to Him." 19 So Samuel grew, and the LORD WAS with him and let none of his words fall to the ground.*

Samuel grew. I love that 19th verse of 1 Samuel 3, don't you? That gives us hope. We can grow in our calling. As Samuel started walking in his calling, the Lord honored him; the Lord was with him and let none of his words fall to the ground. Why? Because he was only speaking the words God was giving him to speak. He was speaking the words of the Lord! He was speaking Truth.

*Isa. 55:11 AMP
So shall My word be that goes forth out of My mouth: it shall not return to Me void [without producing any effect, useless], but it shall accomplish that which I please and purpose, and it shall prosper in the thing for which I sent it.*

We should be very vigilant when speaking forth the prophecy of the Lord. Just listen and speak only what He is saying. I have heard a prophetic word being given on occasion, but it does not stop when God stops!

The same thing can happen with the interpretation of tongues. You can always tell! We are human and God takes that into account. I am not saying this to discourage you from stepping out in your gifts, but I am encouraging you to listen. Your Father will make everything clear. It is not my job to correct; it is only my job to pay attention.

I am very cautious as to whom I allow to speak into my life, or lay hands on me. It is my responsibility to know from God to whom I am to listen and receive. God will let you know. You don't have to sweat it! I am so blessed that He has put apostles and prophets in my life that hear from God clearly! I am so grateful!

God is well able to handle the correction of His children and He does not need our help. I do not correct other people's children, so I often wonder why we as Christians feel it is permissible to correct one another all the time. Of course, when God has given others into our care, then it becomes our duty to correct, but only then! Pastors, for example, are the overseers of our soul. That is why it is so important to be sure we are in the house God wants for us. He tells us where to go, if we will just listen! Ooops......Another "rabbit trail!"

Rom. 1:1 AMP

From Paul, a bondservant of Jesus Christ (the Messiah) called to be an apostle, (a special messenger) set apart to [preach] the Gospel (good news) of and from God,

Eph. 1:4 AMP

Even as [in His love] He chose us [actually picked us out for Himself as His own] in Christ before the foundation of the world, that we should be holy (consecrated and set apart for Him) and blameless in His sight, even above reproach, before Him in love.

As you can see from this scripture, Paul was called. We all know it took some years for Paul to be set apart for his calling. Paul was called before the foundation of the world. Paul was to write a major portion of the New Testament with the Holy Spirit as the true author. God knew it since before Paul was born!

When we know we have a calling, we should be content to prepare ourselves and do just as we are led by the Holy Spirit until we are to be set apart. Exercise patience while waiting on God. This calling can be for any one of the mountains that God has chosen for us. I am not only referring to the Church Mountain! I worked at various jobs until God placed me on my Business Mountain. I did not even know I was called to this particular mountain, but He did! He will make sure you find your place, if you do whatever your hands find to do during the preparation period. We often are being prepared when we are not aware that He is preparing us.

Jude 1 AMP

Jude, A servant of Jesus Christ (the Messiah), and brother of James, [writes this letter] to those
who are called (chosen), dearly loved by God the Father and separated (set apart) and kept for Jesus Christ...

Those of us who are serving Christ in this hour are chosen for this time, and should He desire to set us apart to take one of the Seven Mountains in the Kingdom, then we should embrace it wholeheartedly!

I recommend you study Lance Walnau's teaching on the Seven Mountains. You will gain new insight and realize we were not all called to the Church Mountain in order to do the work of the ministry. I was on the Business

Mountain for over fifty years. At that time I called it my marketplace ministry, because I had not yet received the teaching and revelation of the Seven Mountains.

On a personal note, I have always wanted to write. As a small child I dreamed of being an author. Of course as a child there were many other things I wanted to do as well, but most childish desires wane with age. Writing has never been one of those that grew dim. Only now am I starting to fulfill that God-given heart's desire! I believe I will do more writing, as different ones have prophesied this over me, none of whom knew the vision within me. It is even written in the front of my little Bible that I have used for many years. I did not date it, therefore I do not know when we were asked by a Guest speaker to write in the front of our Bible, something that was a heart's desire that had not yet come to pass. So, on my page it says "To be a `best-selling` author". I have a long, long way to go in fulfilling this desire, I know! But, you see, I needed to make a start. Write the vision down! Start working on it! The Holy Spirit will give us greater anointing and revelation, as we are obedient to our call.

Eph. 4:11-13 AMP
And His gifts were [varied; He Himself appointed and gave men to us] some to be apostles (special messengers),
some prophets (inspired preachers and expounders), some evangelists (preachers of the Gospel, traveling missionaries), some pastors (shepherds of His flock) and teachers. 12 His intention was the perfecting and the full equipping of the saints (His consecrated people), [that they should do] the work of ministering toward building up Christ's body (the church), 13 [That it might develop] until we all attain oneness in the faith and in the comprehension of the [full and accurate] knowledge of the Son of God,

that [we might arrive] at really mature manhood (the completeness of personality which is nothing less than the standard height of Christ's own perfection), the measure of the stature of the fullness of the Christ and the completeness found in Him.

Whatever your calling is, whatever Mountain you are called to possess, embrace it and allow God to set you apart for your work of the ministry, on your Mountain or Mountains.

Running with God is an exciting marathon. Stay in the lane He has designated for you and just see what blessings it will bring. In this race we can and do, win. Run your race boldly!

Heb 12:1 AMP
12:1 THEREFORE THEN, since we are surrounded by so great a cloud of witnesses [who have borne testimony to the Truth], let us strip off and throw aside every encumbrance (unnecessary weight) and that sin which so readily (deftly and cleverly) clings to and entangles us, and let us run with patient endurance and steady and active persistence the appointed course of the race that is set before us,

But God...has a plan

CHAPTER ELEVEN

HELPMEETS:
BEING A GODLY SPOUSE

John 15:9-17 NKJV
"As the Father loved Me, I also have loved you; abide in
you keep My commandments, you will abide in My love, just as I
have kept My Father's commandments and abide in His love.
11 "These things I have spoken to you, that My joy may remain in
you, and that your joy may be full. 12This is My commandment,
that you love one another as I have loved you. 13 Greater love has
no one than this, than to lay down one's life for his friends. 14
You are My friends if you do whatever I command you.
15 No longer do I call you servants, for a servant does
not know what his master is doing; but I have called you
friends, for all things that I heard from My Father I have made
known to you. 16 You did not choose Me, but I chose you and
appointed you that you should go and bear fruit, and that your
fruit should remain, that whatever you ask the Father in My name
He may give you. 17 These things I command you, that you love
one another.

You may wonder why I have included the above scripture in this teaching on marriage.   Well, it is such a beautiful passage and such a great commandment from our Lord, that if implemented in a marriage it will allow all of the other aspects to fall into place.   Your spouse should be your best friend!

Col. 3:18-19 AMP
Wives, be subject to your husbands [subordinate and adapt yourselves to them], as is right and fitting and your proper duty in the Lord. 19 Husbands, love your wives [be affectionate and sympathetic with them] and do not be harsh or bitter or resentful toward them.

Eph. 5:22-26 AMP
Wives, be subject (be submissive and adapt yourselves) to your own husbands as [a service] to the Lord.* 23 For the husband is head of the wife as Christ is the Head of the church, Himself the Savior of [His] body. 24 As the church is subject to Christ, so let wives also be subject in everything to their husbands. 25 Husbands, love your wives, as Christ loved the church and gave Himself up for her, 26 So that He might sanctify her, having cleansed her by the washing of water with the Word. *v.22   (Adapt: accustom yourself to, acclimatize to, get used to, etc.)

In verse 22, there is an interesting point to be made. Paul clarifies that the wife is to be subject to "her own husband." Some years ago there was a teaching going around in the Body of Christ that women were to be subject to and under submission to all men in the church. That is not what the Scripture says at all.

Of course, the Five Fold Ministers are always to

be honored, and all of our brothers are to be respected, but by no means does that suggest that a woman is "subject" to them! I am so grateful to the Lord that He made this very clear in the scripture, aren't you?

This same point is made in 1 Peter 3:1 regarding Submission. Peter is not talking here about the relationship of a pastor or apostle to his congregation, which would not only apply to women, but men as well. Peter is talking about husbands and wives.

1 Peter 3:1-7 AMP

In like manner, you married women, be submissive to your own husbands [subordinate yourselves as being secondary to and dependent on them, and adapt yourselves to them], so that even if any do not obey the Word [of God], they may be won over not by discussion but by the [godly] lives of their wives, 2 When they observe the pure and modest way in which you conduct yourselves, together with your reverence [for your husband; you are to feel for him all that reverence includes: to respect, defer to, revere him — to honor, esteem, appreciate, prize, and, in the human sense, to adore him, that is, to admire, praise, be devoted to, deeply love, and enjoy your husband]. 3 Let not yours be the [merely] external adorning with [elaborate] interweaving and knotting of the hair, the wearing of jewelry, or changes of clothes; 4 But let it be the inward adorning and beauty of the hidden person of the heart, with the incorruptible and unfading charm of a gentle and peaceful spirit, which [is not anxious or wrought up ,but] is very precious in the sight of God. 5 For it was thus that the pious women of old who hoped in God were [accustomed] to beautify themselves and were submissive to their husbands [adapting themselves to them as themselves secondary and dependent upon them]. 6 It was thus that Sarah obeyed Abraham [following his guidance and acknowledging his headship over her by] calling him lord (master, leader, authority). And you are now her true daughters if you do right and let nothing terrify you [not giving way to hysterical fears or letting anxieties unnerve you]. 7 In the same way you married men should live considerately with [your wives], with an intelligent recognition [of the marriage relation], honoring the woman as [physically] the weaker, but [realizing that you] are joint heirs of the grace (God's unmerited favor) of life, in order that your prayers may not be hindered and cut off. [Otherwise you cannot pray effectively.]

There are some in the Body of Christ who use the above scripture to teach that women should not use make-up, or wear jewelry, etc. But if you will notice, it again clarifies itself by using the word "merely," which infers it is all right to do so, but it is not the only thing. It is not the primary thing. That is important!

A wife should not badger her unsaved husband, as this could drive him further away. If you badger him, woman of God, it could take longer to get him into the Kingdom of God. Likewise, a husband should not badger his unsaved wife. Just pray for your spouse's salvation. Do not pray loudly in his or her presence, either. To annoy one another is not God's way, but if we continue to pray, God will take care of the answer!

I recall an incident that occurred a few years ago. A precious sister had asked me to pray for the salvation of her husband. I had been praying for him because he was trying to hinder my sister in her walk with the Lord, and she had asked me to pray about the matter. In prayer, God instructed me to go to their home while he was working and, with the wife, anoint the home with oil as well as items in the home that were directly related to the husband. I called her and we established a suitable time to accomplish this mission.

I took my anointing oil and she and I went through the home together anointing the doorposts and other portions of the house. We then went to their bed and anointed the bedpost, praying over his pillow, mattress, and nightstand. We were both praying in the Spirit, as we anointed everything he might touch. We prayed together, declaring him saved! I left her very encouraged, as we had been obedient to the Lord.

Within a short time, three weeks as I recall, she called to say he asked her if he could go to church with her. Prior to this he was pressuring her and trying to get her not to go to church. We rejoiced together. Her husband gave his life to God, by accepting Jesus as his Savior.

One Sunday morning he came over to me and thanked me for praying. I understood that she had told him how we had been praying for him. He continued to serve God until his passing shortly after my own husband had gone home to be with the Lord. I went to his memorial service and was so blessed to know he was home with Jesus!

Heb. 13:17 AMP
Obey your spiritual leaders and submit to them
[continually recognizing their authority over you], for
they are constantly keeping watch over your souls and guarding
your spiritual welfare, as men who will have
to render an account [of their trust]. [Do your part to] let them
do this with gladness and not with sighing and groaning,
for that would not be profitable to you [either].

Many people do not realize what a responsibility a leader has in watching over the souls of those entrusted to him or her. They will someday have to give account before God of how they kept watch! That is enough to discourage anyone from wanting to be a minister, right? Being a leader is a great responsibility, but if God has placed the five-fold calling upon you, He will give you the grace to fulfill it.

The saved husband is to be the spiritual leader over his household. God will deal with his spiritual leadership as well as your ministers'. Wives are to honor that and listen to their husbands. Husbands have a great responsibility before God for their wives! They are entitled to full support from the wife in wanting to please the Father, fulfilling the plans He has laid out for them.

Eph. 5:33 AMP
However, let each man of you [without exception] love
his wife as [being in a sense] his very own self; and let
the wife see that she respects and reverences her husband
[that she notices him, regards him, honors him, prefers
him, venerates, and esteems him; and that she defers to him,
praises him, and loves and admires him exceedingly].

Eph. 5:22-24 TLB
22 You wives must submit to your husbands'
leadership in the same way you submit to the Lord.
23 For a husband is in charge of his wife in the same way
Christ is in charge of his body the Church. (He gave
his very life to take care of it and be its Savior!) 24 So you wives
must willingly obey your husbands in everything, just as the
Church obeys Christ.

Some independent women do not like this portion of scripture. Some feel it is outdated. God's word is never outdated! It is not up to us to decide that any portion of God's word is not for us. We are not given the option of picking and choosing our Scriptures to our taste. It is not a buffet line, although you would think so at times, the way some Scripture is disregarded.

If a wife will be obedient to God and live according to the scripture, she will be abundantly blessed. Her Father God will see to it. There would be less abuse if the wife would vow to live according to God's plan, rather than her own way. She would be living under her Father's protection. This is my opinion, of course, but I believe the Father would not require a wife to do anything that would prove to be harmful to her wellbeing.

Our God is well able to deal with it, but when a wife takes it into her own hands to do it her way; she is no longer living under the umbrella of protection that her Father God provides. As for men, they need to obey the scriptures, as well. That will ensure that they have a good prayer relationship, and their prayers will not be hindered. We all have our part to play in our relationships!

1 Peter 3:7 AMP

In the same way you married men should live considerately with [your wives], with an intelligent recognition [of the marriage relation], honoring the woman as [physically] the weaker, but [realizing that you] are joint heirs of the grace (God's unmerited favor) of life, in order that your prayers may not be hindered and cut off. [Otherwise you cannot pray effectively.]

1 Cor. 13:1-8 AMP
If I could speak all the languages of earth and of angels,
but didn't love others, I would only be a noisy gong or a clang-
ing cymbal 2 And if I have prophetic powers (the
gift of interpreting the divine will and purpose), and under-
stand all the secret truths and mysteries and possess all
knowledge, and if I have [sufficient] faith so that I can remove
mountains, but have not love (God's love in me) I am nothing (a
useless nobody). 3 Even if I dole out all that I have [to the poor in
providing] food, and if I surrender my body to be burned or in
order that I may glory, but have not love (God's love in me), I
gain nothing. 4 Love endures long and is patient and kind; love
never is envious nor boils over with jealousy, is not boastful or
vainglorious, does not display itself haughtily. 5 It is not
conceited (arrogant and inflated with pride); it is not rude (un-
mannerly) and does not act unbecomingly. Love (God's love in
us) does not insist on its own rights or its own way, for it is not
self-seeking; it is not touchy or fretful or resentful; it takes no
account of the evil done to it [it pays no attention to a suffered
wrong]. 6 It does not rejoice at injustice and unright-
eousness, but rejoices when right and truth prevail. 7 Love
bears up under anything and everything that comes, is ever
ready to believe the best of every person, its hopes are fadeless
under all circumstances, and it endures everything [without
weakening]. 8 Love never fails [never fades out or becomes obso-
lete or comes to an end]

Don't you just love 1 Cor. 13 in the Amplified version? It is so beautiful! It's so beautiful that I just had to
put it in this chapter as well! I want it imbedded in
my heart. If we would all live by this Word of God, we
would have no issues in a marriage relationship or in any
other relationships. Lord, hasten that day!

Mark 11:22-26 AMP
And Jesus, replying, said to them, Have faith in
God [constantly]. 23 Truly I tell you, whoever says to this
mountain, "Be lifted up and thrown into the sea!" and does not
doubt at all in his heart but believes that what he says will take
place, it will be done for him.
24 For this reason I am telling you, whatever you ask
for in prayer, believe (trust and be confident) that it is
granted to you, and you will [get it]. 25 And whenever
you stand praying, if you have anything
against anyone, forgive him and let it drop (leave it, let it go), in
order that your Father Who is in heaven may also forgive you
your [own] failings and shortcomings and let them drop.26 But
if you do not forgive, neither will your Father in heaven forgive
your failings and shortcomings.

The above scripture really does not need a commentary. It is self-explanatory! Re-read the section on forgiveness if you feel the need for more amplification!

2 John 6 AMP
And what this love consists in is this: that we live and walk
in accordance with and guided by His
commandments (His orders, ordinances, precepts, teaching). This is the commandment, as you have heard from the
beginning that you continue to walk in love [guided by it and
following it].

Prov. 21:9 AMP
It is better to dwell in a corner of the housetop [on
the flat oriental roof, exposed to all kinds of weather] than in a
house shared with a nagging, quarrelsome, and faultfinding
woman.

169

Prov. 19:13 AMP
13 A self-confident and foolish son is the [multiplied]
calamity of his father, and the contentions of a wife are like a
continual dripping [of water through a chink in the roof].

Prov. 19:13 NKJV
13 A foolish son is the ruin of his father,
And the contentions of a wife are a continual dripping.

2 Tim. 3:16-17 AMP
Every Scripture is God-breathed (given by His inspiration)
and profitable for instruction, for reproof and conviction of
sin, for correction of error and discipline in obedience,
[and] for training in
righteousness (in holy living, in conformity to God's
will in thought, purpose, and action), 17 So that the man of
God may be complete and proficient, well fitted and
thoroughly equipped for every good work.

It is my desire that these Scriptures have indeed proved to be useful to you. If we apply the Word of
God to our Marriages, we will see contented families. We
will then truly be "Light and Salt" to the world.

But God...has a plan

CHAPTER TWELVE

WALKING OUT YOUR DESTINY

Many are the times that during a very trying day, I have received a phone call from a friend or acquaintance that is in need of prayer. They may call for counsel, but all I can ever offer is Prayer and Scripture, if the request is of a personal nature. I have no illusions of being a Counselor. When these calls come, I must lay aside the bad day I am having and try to help them to the best of my ability with the leading of Holy Spirit. At that moment, my day is forgotten, because God has a bigger job for me to do. When I am finished, I realize that the Holy Spirit has ministered to me Himself. If I receive a call for business advice, I give my opinion, plus prayer and scripture if the call is from a believer!

I have come to realize that I am in a new season of my life. When you have been as active as I have been all these years, it takes a while for that realization to settle in with you. So, I guess what this chapter will be is: How did I get to this season, and what has God done in my life while I have been walking out His Word?

My walk with God started at a young age and the first scripture I learned was:

John 3:16. KJV
"For God so loved the world, that he gave his only begotten Son, that whosoever believeth in him should not perish, but have everlasting life."

I have learned many scriptures during my lifetime. But the ones I tend to rely on the most heavily are those that God has made Rhema to me, rather than Logos. They are the ones that have pulled me through hard times, got my body healed, enabled me spiritually to serve Him. At other times I have received Miracles from God just based on His Logos Word, and I can point back to the Miracle without a specific reference. Still others have come from a Sovereign move of God! I now want to recall some of those different times, and how He has blessed me and enabled me in my walk with Him.

In May of this year, I celebrated seventy years of walking with God! I find that difficult to even type on this page. Young people do not understand, at least I know I did not, the phenomenon of getting older. Our bodies do age. However, our soul, made up of mind, will and emotions, stays at a relatively young age. We will all experience this phenomenon, if we live a long life. It cannot be explained to the young, as it makes no sense to them. It is a thing that can only be understood by experiencing it!

As I grew in the Lord, other verses became significant to me. 1 Cor. 12 was important because some of these gifts had been deposited into me. I had these verses prophesied over me on several occasions.

1 Cor. 12:9-10 NKJV
...to another faith by the same Spirit, to another gifts of healings by the same Spirit, 10 to another the working of miracles, to another prophecy, to another discerning of spirits, to another different kinds of tongues, to another the interpretation of tongues.

As you read my teachings in the previous chapters, I gave you many examples of how God used these gifts through me in my life. It is such a privilege to be used by God to accomplish His will on the earth. It is nothing of us, but ALL of HIM. As my late husband, Rey, used to say, " I am just the mailman." We are only to deliver what has been assigned to us to deliver.

During my younger years at which time I was provider for my children and myself, one particular verse was vital:

Phil. 4:19 NKJV
And my God shall supply all your need according to His riches in glory by Christ Jesus.

Phil. 4:19 AMP
19 And my God will liberally supply (fill to the full) your every need according to His riches in glory in Christ Jesus.

Now at that time, I did not have an Amplified Bible, so I was not able to appropriate the "liberally-fill to the full" part of that scripture; but I did get my needs met.

For many healings over the years, I appropriated the common scripture that we all rely on so heavily:

1 Peter 2:24 NKJV
... who Himself bore our sins in His own body on the tree,
that we, having died to sins, might live for
righteousness —by whose stripes you were healed.

It has only been within the last few years that the Lord referred me to the latter portion of verse 23.

1 Peter 2:23 NIV
When they hurled their insults at him, he did not retaliate; when he suffered, he made no threats. Instead, he entrusted himself to him who judges justly

Now, when I pray that scripture, I include that portion of verse 23 that the Lord showed to me! I paraphrase it to say: "I entrust myself to the One who judges justly, by Whose stripes I was healed."

We serve such a wonderful Lord! During the 1960s, when I suffered from what at that time was referred to as a "nervous breakdown," a different verse was given to me. I would say it repeatedly, because it was short and I could remember it. The medication I was on, and the treatment I was being given, was intended to eradicate my memory.

Isn't that just like the devil? He knew that an excellent memory was one of my "Gifts from God" and he tried to steal it. It was as if God said, "This far, and no further." This is MY verse.

Rom. 8:31 KJV
What shall we then say to these things? If God be for us, who can be against us?

It was just a little card I pulled out of my "Precious Promises" box, but God gave it to me, and it rescued me. I quoted this over and over for weeks and months. His Word will not be returned to us void. It will rescue you and heal you! With me, it was a miraculous event. My healing happened instantaneously; I was totally delivered from the hand of the enemy in that psychiatric ward! The doctor couldn't believe it, but I quit those potent medications he had me on, cold turkey, and I had absolutely no withdrawal symptoms of any kind! I was soooo healed! All glory to God our Father, Jesus, and the Holy Spirit for that miracle in my life. I was in my early 30s and life had seemed hopeless.

But God...has a plan

Later on, as years passed, He just continued to answer my prayers. The salvation of my husband, Rey, whom I married in 1970, was another great milestone. I have heard all the arguments against marrying an unsaved person, and I understand them. To them, it is considered being unequally yoked, but God brought us together. I cannot say that I understand it all theologically to this day. I can only share what God did in my life. I am not recommending this to anyone else, just being factual. You see, God saw the beginning from the end, and He saw Rey saved and serving Him! God honored my heart, which has always been to please Him! He gave me Rey, and then He brought him into the Kingdom.

Sometimes I feel that God must look down on us at times and wonder when we will just trust Him and quit letting the enemy beat up on us for what others consider our past mistakes! God knew Rey had not yet found Him when we were married, but He knew that eventually Rey would serve Him with all of his heart and soul. I had never before seen a more zealous person for God than I did in Rey Soto.

Rey praised God for the rest of his life here on earth, and left with praise for God on his lips. He was a vessel used to bring many souls into the Kingdom, complete with the baptism in the Holy Spirit. That became his sole mission in life: to get everyone "filled to overflowing" with Holy Spirit power and boldness.

My advice to everyone is to listen to the Holy Spirit. He knows all things and will guide you. I believe it is a rare thing for God to move in this way, but I am just telling you what God did for me, in His graciousness and love! God is a Faithful King!

In early 1982, I cried out to God about our financial situation at the car dealership. I knew that God had put us there, and we had worked for Him as best we were able, given the economy at that time. God knew what the economy would be when He instructed us to make this major decision and He was always there for us.

As I related to you earlier, we had a chapel in our dealership, which was the talk of the car business! We saw many people saved and filled in that little chapel.

But it was getting rougher and rougher, and when my Banker asked, "Why do you keep doing this?" I only replied, "Because God told us to do this and, until He releases us, we will be here."

After he left and I was crying out to God, He spoke to me really clearly: "Jeremiah 29:11." I spun around in my office chair and grabbed my little NIV Bible that sat on my credenza and swiftly turned to the verse God had given to me. At that time I was not yet familiar with that verse. It is now MY VERSE! Every verse God gives me from His Word, I claim as my very own!

Jer. 29:11 NIV
11 "For I know the plans I have for you," declares the
Lord, "plans to prosper you and not to harm you, plans to give
you hope and a future."

Oh how I rejoiced in the Lord when I read that verse! I still do. I believe that certain scriptures become to us like one of our children. It has been birthed in us, and we claim it for our very own, forever!

I shared the revelation God gave me on the following special scripture as I was preparing a teaching and how it literally leapt off the page at me. He showed it to me as an inner vision. I also previously shared with you how I saw a check that needed a counter-signature to be negotiable, but God had already signed it. It was then up to the recipient to counter-sign with Him. Coming into agreement with Him is such an important step for us to take! It made an indelible mark on my heart that will never leave!

2 Cor. 1:20-21 NIV
For no matter how many promises God has made, they are "Yes"
in Christ. And so through him the "Amen" is spoken by us to
the glory of God.

Again, that is My Verse! That verse has strengthened my faith many times for any number of things I had believed God to produce in my life. God told me things, which were His promises to me, and I just go back to this verse and stand firm as He has instructed us.

Eph. 6:13 NKJV
Therefore take up the whole armor of God, that you may be able to
withstand in the evil day, and having done all, to stand.

You may ask me, Loi, why do you keep saying the same things over again and use the same scriptures over and over? Well, like I said, these verses become like one of your children. They have been birthed in you. You don't just talk about your children once and then never again. No, you talk about them a lot. You share them with anyone who will listen. These scriptures have been birthed in me, and I cannot help but keep sharing them!

It is by communing with Father (Daddy to me, also) that we are given these special times, with special insights and answers to our problems. He is such a loving Daddy, that it makes me proud to be His daughter. We are not prideful for ourselves, but only in Him and for the great privilege of belonging to Him. Holy Spirit tells us things, and we need His discerning to know what to share and what is to be saved for another time. Sometimes the Holy Spirit will share information with us that is not to be repeated, things for us to ponder and pray about.

In 1994, our step-grandson was killed. It should not have happened, but it did! He was very precious to me, as the Father God had created a special bond between us. If he needed to call me for prayer, he knew he could call. The time of day was of no consequence. That was our special relationship. I always said he was the only person who could get away with calling me at three o'clock in the morning, and he did. I had seen him and we had prayed and fellowshipped together just 10 days before he was killed.

There was no subject that was off-limits for

John. I loved that young man dearly, and it was an unrighteous act that took his life, but Father God knew all that! The following scripture became very important to me and Rey, who also loved him like a son. We knew he was with his Heavenly Father, and we drew much comfort from that fact. We also forgave the man who was responsible for John's death, and I still pray that he will give his life to Jesus, although I no longer remember his name.

Isa. 57:1-2 AMP
The Righteous man perishes, and no one lays it to
heart; and merciful and devout men are taken away, with no one
considering that the uncompromisingly upright and godly person
is taken away from the calamity and evil to come [even through
wickedness].
2 He [in death] enters into peace; they rest in their beds, each
one who walks straight and in his uprightness.

Rey and I held Bible studies in our home for over twenty years. They were more like Bible fellowships, actually, since food was also served. Rey knew that people were better listeners and participation was greater if the people were doing it on a satisfied stomach! He always announced it as "snacks," but it was always a full meal. We had in attendance one person to one hundred on any given night. But we averaged around thirty people each week. We called them our "regulars".

We started doing this on a Thursday night in the beginning, as our midweek church service was on Wednesdays. When our church changed mid-week service from Wednesday to Thursday, we changed our night to Friday. Then when our church service moved to Friday night, we moved Bible study back to Wednesday, and there it remained until we ceased having them in 2003, just before

Rey went home to be with Jesus.

We saw many lives changed over those twenty years. I remember one particular night, the food was all prepared, and no one had come. We were seeking the Lord as to whether it had come time to close the study sessions. We said, "Lord, if no one comes tonight, we will know You want us to cease with this Bible study." That was approximately eight years from the time it had started. We just waited on God, when suddenly one young woman came in saying, "Sorry to be so late, as I hadn't planned to come, but just felt prompted by the Holy Spirit that I needed to be here!" We had a glorious time that night, I might add! We never questioned again, and our attendance was very consistent in numbers.

We had all sorts of people from so-called "big names" to so-called "little people," but the Spirit of God moved among us all the same! There are neither "big names" nor "little people" in God's eyes. It is as thrilling when a six year old is filled with the Holy Spirit as it is for an adult. Rey thrived on children receiving from Jesus!

I remember the Wednesday that God gave Rey a special assignment for flash cards to demonstrate how the Holy Spirit worked when we prayed in the Spirit. He did not know the reason, but he was obedient to the Lord. Rey always set aside Wednesdays to listen to direction from God as to how many to prepare food for, both physically and spiritually. So he was prepared with lots of food on both fronts! That night three or four young men from the USC football team attended, and they ate to their hearts' content. The flash cards made such an impact on them that they all received what God had prepared: the infilling of The Holy Spirit for some and a re-fill for others, but they all received interpretation and were greatly edified. God is so good!

Many people talk fondly about those Bible study days, but everything has its season. One young woman, who is very precious to me, recently told me that Wednesday night Bible study was like "family night!" How precious is that?

Another scripture that has always been important to me is in Ephesians.

Eph. 2:10 NIV
"For we are God's workmanship, created in Christ Jesus to do good works, which God prepared in advance for us to do."

I have always found this verse to be so comforting over the years, just knowing that God has everything planned out in advance for me. It has carried me through the times I have questioned, because I am not a dynamic speaker like some of my friends and acquaintances. I tend to be very soft spoken and I think of how marvelous it would be to speak with such a strong fiery voice as many of the other female Christian leaders.

When Kaye got her two new kidneys, it was in response to my soft-spoken invitation, and the Lord let me know that is how He made me, and it was all for His purpose for me! I have never questioned Him since that day, and it has allowed me to give more grace to speakers that are not as dynamic as others. It is not how loud nor soft, slow in speaking, or fast paced; but it is about what are we doing with the gift God has put in us. Are we doing what He has called us to do?

I related to you earlier how from a small child, I learned to "measure my words. " Think before speaking!

I realized at a young age that doing so would make me more acceptable and allow me to have a roof over my head. People did not want to take in a child that was onerous! It was only with Mother Potter that I had the confidence to be more outspoken. I was not concerned with being "sent away."

I always get a smile when I remember the first time Mother Potter thought I was being "sassy." I hastened to inform her that I was not sassing her, but that we all had Freedom of Speech. I learned then that even Freedom of Speech has its limitations!

In looking back over my life, I can see a common thread of when it was me talking out of my intellect, or when I was speaking what God was putting into my spirit by the Holy Spirit! It is truly an amazing thing, and I am sure that as you reach an age when you start evaluating, you will also see a common thread as to how The Holy Spirit has spoken through you.

Now I am not talking only about spiritual encounters, but in the everyday, grind-it-out world of life. In your business situations, Holy Spirit is right there to give you input, so you have proper output. He has made me look smart many, many times in my fifty-plus years in business. However, as He told me when he trained me for the car business, "You can take the credit, as long as you give Me the glory." Actually, I know to whom all credit and glory is due for my life. He is my King of Kings and my Lord of Lords!

My precious Rey went to be with the most important one in his life in October, 2003. I was the most important one to him until July 5, 1978, when he came to know Jesus and His Holy Spirit, who introduced him to the Father. I was always very happy to be second to Them!

Rey did not have to linger and suffer as so many do. I am grateful to my Lord for that! It was so fitting that he went home in October, as October had always been "our month." Both our birthdays were in October, as well as our closest buddies from the old days, Carl and Gail. We always celebrated the whole month! Carl and Gail were both already home with Jesus when Rey joined them over there, so the October celebration just got a whole lot bigger and better!

Sixteen months after Rey went Home, my first-born, Zoe Leeta, also went Home to be with Jesus. My precious Daddy God gave me the grace to get through those days with peace, and then He restored my joy! As a dear brother once said in his sermon: "God can pull you through anything, if you can stand the pulling." I am so thankful that He did the pulling for me, and I learned more from Him in the process.

If I tried to cover everything God has done in my life, I would never get this book finished, so necessity dictates that I must leave out a significant number of experiences and lessons. My prayer is that there is something between these book covers that will help you with your own personal walk with God. So just walk out your life as He has ordained it, which I have tried to do and am still working on doing. Allow Him to bring you into your destiny. It truly is a "walking out" of The Word in your life that really matters. Nothing else is worthwhile!

The year was 1990, and I was sitting at my desk in my office when the call came. It was my cousin, calling to say that Mama Potter had suffered a cerebral hemorrhage and was in a coma.

I immediately called Rey to let him know that I was making plane reservations and would be home shortly to pack a few things for my trip. KJ wanted to accompany me, to be with her grandmother. I had arranged for a rental car to drive from Will Rogers Airport in Oklahoma City, to my hometown of Thomas.

When we arrived at the hospital they advised me she was in a coma and was not responding. I walked into her room and over to her bedside, and kissed her on the cheek. I said, "I love you, Mama." She immediately opened her eyes, raised her head slightly, and smiled at me, saying, "I knew you would come." She then lay back, closed her eyes, and was again comatose.

The doctor came in to speak to me and the other relatives that were there. Her sisters and nieces had been by her side while I was traveling. The Doctor advised us that we might as well go get some rest, as she would be in that state for possibly a long period. He stated that it could be weeks, months or even years for that kind of coma. Suddenly, in a strong voice, I proclaimed, "No! She will not! She will either be healed here and now or go home to Jesus for her reward." He looked at me and walked away.

I was holding Mama in my arms, and her spirit left for Heaven. I sensed it when she left, as though a feather was floating toward Heaven. This was before the doctor had even made it to the front door of the hospital, which was a short distance, since Thomas Hospital was a small hospital. He was shocked, since all of her vital signs had been strong, even though she had the brain hemorrhage.

I knew Mama did not want to lie in a hospital bed for an extended time, and she had been speaking of looking forward to dancing with Daddy on the streets of gold.

Daddy had gone home several years before, and now was her time to go home! She was eighty years young when she left us. She had her dress already made, and she called it her "Coronation" gown. She had her celebration songs all selected for her Memorial Celebration, one of which was that "peppy" Pentecostal song, "I'm Living On The Hallelujah Side". She had everything in order for this last journey. I still miss her so much! I miss her love and her Godly advice, which she so freely gave, but only when asked.

In 1992 the Lord gave me a song, "Thank You Jesus for Introducing Me to the Father." He just gave it to me as I was praising Him driving to a business meeting.

I am so grateful that Jesus made that introduction to Father, in my life!

If I have shared the same things too many times, forgive me. These particular incidents were such milestones for me that I felt the need to repeat them.

Jer. 29:11 NIV
"For I know the plans I have for you," declares the LORD,"
plans to prosper you and not to harm you, plans to give you hope and a future."

Eph. 2:10 NIV
For we are God's workmanship, created in Christ Jesus to do good works, which God prepared in advance for us to do

Let us go forward, take our mountain, and fulfill our destiny! Embrace God's plan and travel on every Rabbit Trail that He takes you on, knowing that He will always get you to your destination on time!

God Has Always Had A Plan

3 John 2 AMP

2 Beloved, I pray that you may prosper in every way and [that your body] may keep well, even as [I know] your soul keeps well and prospers.

God Has Always Had A Plan

Eph. 2:10 AMP
For we are God's [own] handiwork (His workmanship),recreated in Christ Jesus, [born anew]
that we may do those good works which God predestined (planned beforehand) for us [taking paths which He prepared ahead of time], that we should walk in them [living the good life which He prearranged and made ready for us to live].

Other books available from
Kingdom Enterprises International
& Destiny Center at
# www.DestinyCenter.com

Non-Fiction Books:
In My Father's Hands by Bunty Bunce
The Great Eagle Calling by Millie Toms
Rabbit Trails by Lois Lee Soto

by Diane Wigstone
Happily Single: Before Happily Married
Hope for Hollywood: Reclaiming the Soul of Film & TV
14 Generations: America's Critical Choice for
Blessing or Exile

Coming Soon by Diane Wigstone:
Discovering Your Destiny
Doing Your Destiny
*Discipling the Nations through Arts, Media &
Entertainment*

Other resources available from
Kingdom Enterprises International
& Destiny Center at
# www.DestinyCenter.com

Kingdom Romance Novels by
Elizabeth W. Drake including:
The Corporate Escape
Maid of Honor
Chéri Amour

ⴡⴟ

Movie DVD, Cd & MP3's
Crossroads Cafe -
Movie DVD, Soundtrack Cd
& MP3's

Kiowa Legacy -
Documentary DVD

Training DVD's
Public Speaking: Platform 101 - Training DVD
Discovering Your Destiny - Training DVD
Movies & Training Church Viewing License through
www.ChurchMovieNight.com

Jewelry Companies
www.JusticeGems.com
www.KingdomCollection.com

Website & Domain Services
www.DomainsDNA.com

22071720R00104

Made in the USA
Charleston, SC
09 September 2013